INTERNATIONAL DEVELOPMENT IN FOCUS

Breathing Heavy
New Evidence on Air Pollution and Health in Bangladesh

WAMEQ AZFAR RAZA, IFFAT MAHMUD, AND
TAMER SAMAH RABIE

WORLD BANK GROUP

Contents

Figures

Maps

Tables

Acknowledgments

The authors of the report are indebted to the Bangladesh Department of Environment of the Ministry of Environment, Forest, and Climate Change, for sharing data on air pollution levels in Bangladesh. The authors would like to recognize the team members of the Development Research Initiative who collected data for the survey, specifically Mr. Mamun Rashid and Dr. Munshi Sulaiman. The authors gratefully acknowledge contributions from Ms. Aneire Khan and Mr. Jyotirmoy Saha. The authors are also grateful for the collaboration extended by Prof. Dr. Md. Delwar Hossain, Head of Respiratory Medicine, and Dr. Ishmum Zia Chowdhury, BIRDEM Hospital and Ibrahim Medical College.

The authors gratefully acknowledge the time provided by Prof. Tahmina Shirin, Director of the Institute of Epidemiology and Disease Control Research of the Ministry of Health and Family Welfare of the Government of Bangladesh, and Mr. Md. Ziaul Haque, Director of Air Quality Management, Department of Environment of the Ministry of Environment, Forest, and Climate Change, who reviewed the draft report before its finalization.

The authors express their gratitude to the peer reviewers Mr. Stephen Geoffrey Dorey (Senior Health Specialist), Mr. Jostein Nygard (Senior Environmental Specialist), and Mr. Muthukumara Mani (Lead Economist), as well as Mr. Iqbal Ahmed (Senior Environmental Specialist), Mr. M. Khaliquzzaman (Senior Environmental Consultant), and Ms. Ana Luisa Gomes Lima (Senior Environmental Specialist) at the World Bank for their valuable comments. The authors are grateful to Ms. Dandan Chen, Acting Country Director for Bangladesh and Bhutan, World Bank, who chaired an internal review meeting to seek expert input for finalization of the report.

The authors are grateful for the financial support from the Health Sector Support Project Multi-Donor Trust Fund, which is cofinanced by the Embassy of the Kingdom of the Netherlands; the Foreign, Commonwealth, and Development Office of the United Kingdom; Gavi, the Vaccine Alliance; Global Affairs Canada; and the Swedish Development Cooperation Agency.

About the Authors

Iffat Mahmud is a Public Policy Practitioner focusing on human development. She has more than 15 years of experience in South Asia and Western Africa, particularly in Bangladesh, India, Nepal, Pakistan, Tanzania, and Uganda, leading project management and policy dialogue with governments and partners. Her expertise is in advising public sector institutions on policies, strategies, and interventions; managing projects; and undertaking analytics. Her work spans a wide range of themes, including maternal and child health, nutrition, communicable diseases, health service delivery, institutional reforms, systems development, and emergency response. Her work includes such cross-cutting areas as climate change, water and sanitation, and social protection. She is a Senior Operations Officer at the Health, Nutrition and Population Global Practice of the World Bank. She obtained her master of science degree in management and bachelor of science in economics from the London School of Economics and Political Science.

Tamer Samah Rabie is a Lead Health Specialist in the World Bank's Health, Nutrition and Population Global Practice. He is a medical doctor with a master's degree in public health from the London School of Hygiene and Tropical Medicine. He has over 25 years of experience spanning clinical medicine, public health, health systems, health policy, service delivery, infectious diseases, nutrition, governance, the private sector, and environmental health. Since joining the World Bank in 2005, he has led lending as well as advisory services programs in over 25 countries in Europe and Central Asia, South Asia, East Asia, and the Middle East and North Africa regions. Further, he has developed analytical and knowledge products in several areas in the health field. In 2019, he established the Health Climate and Environment Program—which he currently leads—with the aim to integrate environmental health and climate-smart health care measures into World Bank operations.

Wameq Azfar Raza is a Health and Nutrition Specialist with the World Bank's Health, Nutrition and Population Global Practice in Bangladesh. Before this, he served as a Poverty Economist with the Poverty and Equity Global Practice. He is an applied microeconomist with national and international experience in analytical work, program design, and implementation across eight countries in

Asia and Sub-Saharan Africa. His work includes areas such as health and nutrition, social protection, and ultrapoverty interventions. He has published peer-reviewed articles in leading journals in the economics and health fields. He holds a master's degree in development economics from the University of Sussex and a doctorate in health economics from Erasmus University Rotterdam.

Main Messages

Bangladesh is highly vulnerable to the effects of air pollution. It has been ranked as the most polluted country in the world; its capital, Dhaka, has been ranked as the second-most polluted city in the world between 2018 and 2021 (IQAir 2021). Air pollution was the second-largest risk factor, causing most deaths and disability in Bangladesh in 2019. An estimated 78,145 to 88,229 deaths and 1.0 billion to 1.1 billion days lived with illness in Bangladesh in 2019 were attributable to ambient air pollution (World Bank, forthcoming). The associated economic losses are considerable, estimated between 3.9 and 4.4 percent of the country's gross domestic product during the same year.

Sufficient evidence is available globally to establish the relationship between air pollution and adverse health effects; the information specific to Bangladesh is, however, sparse. Accordingly, there is a need to better understand the air pollution levels in the country and document their interaction with human health. This report, one of the first of its kind from Bangladesh, seeks to establish the relationship between ambient air pollution and the associated short-term health impacts. It uses household-level data collected from 12,250 individuals, stratified by sources of ambient air pollution chosen from Dhaka and rural Sylhet reflecting varying concentration levels of air pollutants. The report uses fine particulate matter ($PM_{2.5}$) to track exposure to outdoor air pollution, because it is considered the most harmful to human health among the air pollutants of major public health concern identified by the World Health Organization (WHO).

Key highlights of the report are as follows:

- **Air pollution levels within the country vary significantly, with the western regions (Khulna and Rajshahi) more polluted than the eastern ones (Sylhet and Chattogram).** Dhaka is the most polluted division, while Sylhet is the least polluted (based on average $PM_{2.5}$ levels recorded by the Department of Environment [DoE] between 2013 and 2021). Moreover, historical analysis of the data between 2013 and 2021 from the DoE suggests that the air pollution levels in Dhaka have become increasingly concentrated, while they have been dissipating in Sylhet over the years.

- **The highest concentrations of pollution in urban Bangladesh are found in sites with major construction and persistent traffic, followed by sites with brick kilns.** The highest $PM_{2.5}$ concentration levels, as per the data collected during the dry season for this study, were recorded in locations with major construction and persistent traffic; these levels were approximately 150 percent above the WHO Air Quality Guidelines (AQG) 2021, equivalent to smoking 1.7 cigarettes per day (Echenique 2018). The second-highest concentration of $PM_{2.5}$ levels were in locations near brick kilns, with an average exposure of 136 percent above the WHO AQG 2021, or equivalent to smoking 1.6 cigarettes per day. This finding is in comparison to rural Sylhet, considered the least polluted region in the country, where, worryingly, the $PM_{2.5}$ exposure levels were 80 percent above WHO's AQG 2021, or equivalent to smoking 1.2 cigarettes per day.

- **The report establishes a direct association between ambient air pollution and human health.** Exposure to $PM_{2.5}$ is significantly and positively associated with breathing difficulties, cough, and lower respiratory tract infections. A 1 percent increase in exposure to $PM_{2.5}$ over WHO's 2021 AQG is associated with a 12.8 percent increase in the probability of a person experiencing breathing difficulties, 12.5 percent for cough, and 8.1 percent for lower respiratory tract infection.

- **Most vulnerable to the effects of air pollution are the elderly (ages 65 years or more), children (ages 0 to 5 years), and people with comorbidities.** Cough and breathing difficulties—conditions typically associated with air pollution—were highest among these groups, after controlling for several confounding factors, including demographic and socioeconomic characteristics, as well as comorbidities experienced by the individual. Moreover, comparison across sites reveals that lower respiratory tract infections were the highest among children and the elderly living in locations with major construction and traffic than in locations with brick kilns and persistent traffic and in the comparator site. People with underlying health conditions such as allergies, diabetes, and hypertension, and those who live in areas with major construction and traffic, are similarly more likely to experience lower respiratory tract infections than those living in other locations.

The government of Bangladesh has policies and measures in place to mitigate the impacts of air pollution. The 2012 Air Pollution Reduction Strategy for Bangladesh stipulates strategies to reduce emission levels, promote use of improved technologies to improve air quality, and undertake institutional reforms to improve coordination and governance. In addition, a Clean Air Bill was drafted in 2019 that will facilitate preparation of the National Air Quality Management Plan and identify critical areas to improve air quality (HEI 2020). In September 2021, the government released the Mujib Climate Prosperity Plan Decade 2030, which shifts the discourse on climate change from "vulnerability to resilience to prosperity" for Bangladesh.

Climate change and air pollution interact with each other—climate variables (temperature, surface pressure, and relative humidity) and air pollutants act together and aggravate climate change. Climate change is projected to worsen in Bangladesh and to be aggravated by contributing factors like urbanization; as a result, air pollution levels are likely to intensify over time. Hence, there is an urgent need for the health sector to be better prepared to deal with the impending crisis. The primary evidence derived from this report underscores the need for the following important steps:

- Improving health service delivery platforms to deal with air pollution–related mortality and morbidity, with a focus on vulnerable populations, such as the elderly and children
- Strengthening the public health response mechanism
- Expanding the scope and accuracy of the air pollution data captured, not only to better track a rapidly evolving situation, but also to formulate effective responses to related and emerging health issues
- Engaging in further research to improve the understanding on the topic and devising measures to effectively address the impacts of air pollution.

REFERENCES

Echenique, Martin. 2018. "How Much Are You 'Smoking' by Breathing Urban Air?" *Bloomberg*, April 25. https://www.bloomberg.com/news/articles/2018-04-25/the-app-that -translates-air-pollution-into-cigarettes.

HEI (Health Effects Institute). 2020. *State of Global Air 2020: Special Report*. Boston, MA: Health Effects Institute.

IQAir. 2021. *World Air Quality Report: Region and City PM$_{2.5}$ Ranking*. Goldach, Switzerland: IQAir. https://www.iqair.com/bangladesh/dhaka.

World Bank. Forthcoming. *Building Back a Greener Bangladesh: Country Environmental Analysis*. Washington, DC: World Bank.

Executive Summary

Air pollution was the fourth-leading risk factor for premature mortality globally in 2019, causing an estimated 6.67 million deaths (HEI 2020). A large majority of such deaths were caused by ambient, outdoor air pollution due to inhalation of fine particulate matter ($PM_{2.5}$) (World Bank 2020). While most individuals are susceptible to the health effects of air pollution, those living in low- and middle-income countries are most impacted by "unbreathable" air as they are exposed to very high levels of air pollution, typically exceeding the safe limits set by the World Health Organization (WHO 2022). Bangladesh is particularly vulnerable to the effects of air pollution—the country has been ranked as the most polluted in the world between 2018 and 2021. Dhaka, its capital, has ranked as the second-most polluted city in the world over the same period (IQAir 2021).

Air pollution was the second-largest risk factor that caused most deaths and disability in Bangladesh in 2019, with four of the top five causes of total deaths in the country being directly associated with air pollution: stroke, ischemic heart disease, chronic obstructive pulmonary disease, and lower respiratory tract infection (HEI 2020). An estimated 78,145 to 88,229 deaths and 1.0 billion to 1.1 billion days lived with illness in Bangladesh in 2019 were attributable to ambient air pollution (World Bank, forthcoming). The economic losses incurred due to these adverse effects are considerable, estimated between 3.9 and 4.4 percent of the country's gross domestic product during the same year.

WHO identifies at least six air pollutants of major public health concern: fine particulate matter ($PM_{2.5}$), coarse particulate matter (PM_{10}), ozone at ground level (O_3, not the ozone layer in the upper atmosphere), nitrogen dioxide (NO_2), sulfur dioxide (SO_2), and carbon monoxide (CO). Of these, $PM_{2.5}$ is considered the most harmful for human health and is known to cause several health issues. Because of its microscopic size, $PM_{2.5}$ can pass through the nose and get into the bloodstream through the lungs, affecting all major human organs. (PM numbers indicate the size of particles: $PM_{2.5}$ indicates particles of 2.5 micrometers, and so forth.) Short- and long-term diseases caused by exposure to $PM_{2.5}$ are related to the cardiovascular and respiratory systems, often worsening existing health conditions like asthma, bronchitis, and lung cancer.

There is a synergistic relationship between climate change and air pollution—climate variables (temperature, surface pressure, and relative humidity) and air pollutants interact and contribute to climate change. Emission of greenhouse gases (such as carbon dioxide and ozone), PM from burning of fossil fuels, and extreme weather conditions like heat waves and drought due to global warming worsen the quality of air. It is likely that climate change will significantly aggravate air pollution, particularly in densely populated areas (Orru, Ebi, and Forsberg 2017).

Although there is considerable global evidence that establishes the relationship between air pollution and adverse health effects, information specific to Bangladesh is sparse. Moreover, the available evidence is constrained due to limitations in geographical coverage of studies, the fact that they were conducted with small nonrepresentative samples, or a lack of localized granular air pollution data that can effectively link the impact of air pollution on health. Hence, there is a need to better understand the air pollution levels in the country and document their interaction with human health.

This report uses data collected from 12,250 individuals, stratified by sources of ambient air pollution chosen from Dhaka and rural Sylhet reflecting varying concentration levels of air pollutants. These include sites in Dhaka city covering locations (in Dhaka city) with major construction and traffic, sites (in Dhaka city) with persistent traffic (no construction), sites (in the outskirts of Dhaka) capturing locations with brick kilns, and sites (in rural Sylhet) as the comparator. The survey collected information on individuals' physical and mental health conditions, household-level background information, and air pollution data, localized at the community and household levels. Analysis of the primary data was complemented by an analysis of existing literature and historical data on air pollution levels from across the country. This report, one of the first of its kind from Bangladesh, aims to establish the relationship between ambient air pollution and the associated short-term health impacts.

Key highlights of the report are the following:

- ***Air pollution levels within the country vary significantly, with the western regions (Khulna and Rajshahi) more polluted than the eastern ones (Sylhet and Chattogram).*** Dhaka is the most polluted division, while Sylhet the least polluted (based on average $PM_{2.5}$ levels recorded by the Department of Environment [DoE] between 2013 and 2021). Moreover, historical analysis of the data between 2013 and 2021 from the DoE suggests that the air pollution levels in Dhaka are becoming increasingly concentrated, while they have been dissipating in Sylhet over the years.

- ***The highest concentrations of pollution in urban Bangladesh are found in sites with major construction and persistent traffic, followed by sites with brick kilns.*** The highest $PM_{2.5}$ concentration levels, as per the data collected during the dry season for this study, were recorded in locations with major construction and persistent traffic, approximately 150 percent above the World Health Organization (WHO) Air Quality Guidelines (AQG) 2021, equivalent to smoking 1.7 cigarettes per day (Echenique 2018). The second-highest concentration $PM_{2.5}$ levels were in locations near brick kilns, with an average exposure of 136 percent above the WHO AQG 2021, or equivalent to smoking 1.6 cigarettes per day. This is in comparison to rural Sylhet, considered the least polluted region in the country, where, worryingly, the $PM_{2.5}$ exposure levels were 80 percent above WHO's AQG 2021, or equivalent to smoking 1.2 cigarettes per day.

- ***The report establishes a direct association between ambient air pollution and human health.*** Exposure to $PM_{2.5}$ is significantly and positively associated with experiencing breathing difficulties, cough, and lower respiratory tract infections. A 1 percent increase in exposure to $PM_{2.5}$ over WHO's AQG 2021 is associated with a 12.8 percent increase in the probability of a person experiencing breathing difficulties, 12.5 percent for cough, and 8.1 percent for lower respiratory tract infection.
- ***Most vulnerable to the effects of air pollution are the elderly (ages 65 years or more), children (ages 0 to 5 years), and people with comorbidities.*** Cough and breathing difficulties—conditions typically associated with air pollution—were highest among these groups, after controlling for several confounding factors, including demographic and socioeconomic characteristics as well as comorbidities being experienced by the individual. Moreover, comparison across sites reveals that lower respiratory tract infections were the highest among children and the elderly living in locations with major construction and traffic than in locations with brick kilns and persistent traffic and in the comparator site. People with underlying health conditions such as allergies, diabetes, and hypertension, and those who live in areas with major construction and traffic, are similarly more likely to experience lower respiratory tract infections than those living in any other location.

The government of Bangladesh has policies and measures in place to mitigate the impacts of air pollution. The 2012 Air Pollution Reduction Strategy for Bangladesh stipulates strategies to reduce emission levels, promote use of improved technologies to improve air quality, and undertake institutional reforms to improve coordination and governance. In addition, a Clean Air Bill was drafted in 2019 that will facilitate preparation of the National Air Quality Management Plan and identify critical areas to improve air quality (HEI 2020). In September 2021, the government released the Mujib Climate Prosperity Plan Decade 2030, which shifts the discourse on climate change from "vulnerability to resilience to prosperity" for Bangladesh. Priority areas and points emphasized by the plan are (1) accelerating adaptation to the effects of climate change; (2) transitioning from the use of manual labor to advanced technology and future-proofing industry with technology transfer; (3) increasing public revenue to spend on the most vulnerable populations; (4) undertaking comprehensive climate and disaster risk financing and management; (5) leveraging twenty-first-century technologies for well-being; and (6) maximizing renewable energy, energy efficiency, and power and transportation sector resilience.

Driven by climate change and compounded by contributing factors like urbanization, air pollution levels are likely to intensify further over time. Hence, there is an urgent need for the health sector to be better prepared to deal with the impending crisis. The primary evidence derived from this report underscores the need for the following:

- ***Improving health service delivery platforms to deal with air pollution–related mortality and morbidity, with a focus on vulnerable populations, such as the elderly and children.*** Curative services need to be further improved to deal with the health impacts. This would also entail strengthening the capacity and awareness of health professionals.
- ***Strengthening the public health response mechanism.*** Community-level screening for specific health conditions associated with air pollution

(like cough and breathing difficulties) among people living in areas with relatively high air pollution (such as major construction sites and persistent traffic) will assist the government in early detection and facilitate responses to emerging health issues. In addition, outreach activities can raise awareness of potential health risks due to air pollution and promote healthy lifestyle choices.

- *Expanding the scope and accuracy of the air pollution data captured, not only to better track a rapidly evolving situation, but also to formulate effective responses to related and emerging health issues.* Installation of additional continuous air monitoring stations to the existing fleet of 13 stations is needed to collect more localized and granular information on the air pollutants. If the installation of the additional stations is coupled with regular tracking of weather data (on temperature, humidity, precipitation, and surface pressure) by the Bangladesh Meteorological Department, it would be possible to make detailed air quality assessments across the country and determine the impact of air pollution.

- *Engaging in further research to improve the understanding on the topic and devising measures to effectively address the impacts of air pollution.* Potential areas can include the nexus between climate change and air pollution, assessment of all preexisting health conditions that can be aggravated by air pollution, association between air pollution and coronavirus disease (COVID-19) to understand the influence and trajectory of climate change, and the potential effect of immunization in reducing morbidity due to air pollution.

With air pollution levels anticipated to increase in the coming years, the negative effects on individuals will continue to amplify, thereby increasing the national burden and cost of care in the medium to long term. More specifically, to deal with the issues highlighted in this report, options for public intervention are presented in table ES.1 The findings and recommendations contained in this report are expected to assist practitioners and subject matter experts in policy dialogue under the overall framework of the government's Mujib Climate Prosperity Plan Decade 2030.

TABLE ES.1 **Matrix of policy options**

	THE MINISTRY OF HEALTH AND FAMILY WELFARE AT THE LEAD, IN COLLABORATION WITH RELEVANT MINISTRIES, LOCAL GOVERNMENT, AND OTHER STAKEHOLDERS	
Adaptive measures for the health sector	*Policy recommendation 1* Improve health service delivery to deal with the health effects of air pollution, with a focus on vulnerable populations such as the elderly and children.	**Actions**
		• Increase awareness and sensitivity of health care professionals on the health risks associated with exposure to ambient air pollution.
		• Enhance the capacity of medical practitioners through targeted training to detect and treat air-pollution-driven morbidity.
		• Institute a mainstream response to deal with mental health issues through the provision of community-based solutions for prevention and treatment (for instance, the creation of peer support groups).
		• Train nonspecialists to detect and treat common mental disorders.
	Policy recommendation 2 Strengthen the public health response mechanism to promote preventive measures.	• Establish community-level mobile teams to screen for health risks associated with air pollution. These teams should work in shifts and be available during the evening to cover the population not available during the daytime.
		• Prioritize the screening of the elderly and children, who are more susceptible to the effects of air pollution.
		• Create awareness among the general population about the adverse effects on health due to air pollution through outreach activities using community health workers and volunteers.
		• Mobilize communities, local leaders, and social influencers to promote preventive actions such as regular use of face masks, which can reduce inhalation of harmful pollutants to an extent.
		• Identify areas with relatively high air pollution as "hot spots" where these actions need to be prioritized.
	THE MINISTRY OF ENVIRONMENT, FOREST, AND CLIMATE CHANGE CAN LEAD, IN CONSULTATION WITH THE RELEVANT MINISTRIES AND STAKEHOLDERS	
Adaptive measures through a multisectoral approach	*Policy recommendation 3* Record more granular and localized data with high fidelity to monitor air pollution levels closely.	**Actions**
		• Increase the number of continuous air-monitoring stations throughout the country to be able to collect more localized and granular information on the various air pollutants.
		• Strengthen capacity to capture additional data points using updated technology.
		• Use existing sources of information, coupled with localized ground-level information, to continually monitor the impact of air pollution on human health.
		• Establish effective public outreach systems to provide early warning during days expected to have high air pollution levels.
	Policy recommendation 4 Conduct further research to substantiate the effects of air pollution on health as well to establish the nexus between climate change and air pollution.	• Collect repeated time-series data on air pollution as well as on specific health issues that are influenced by air pollution, from a larger sample over a longer time horizon.
		• Undertake analytical work to investigate issues such as the association between air pollution and COVID-19; substantiate the nexus between climate change and air pollution; analyze the effects of preexisting health conditions that can be exacerbated due to exposure; and study the effect of immunization such as pneumococcal vaccines among children in reducing morbidity precipitated by air pollution.
		• Set up mechanisms to make available research grants and/or innovation funds to encourage technical work.

REFERENCES

Echenique, Martin. 2018. "How Much Are You 'Smoking' by Breathing Urban Air?" *Bloomberg*, April 25. https://www.bloomberg.com/news/articles/2018-04-25/the-app -that-translates-air-pollution-into-cigarettes.

HEI (Health Effects Institute). 2020. *State of Global Air 2020: Special Report*. Boston, MA: Health Effects Institute.

IQAir. 2021. *World Air Quality Report: Region and City PM$_{2.5}$ Ranking*. Goldach, Switzerland: IQAir. https://www.iqair.com/bangladesh/dhaka.

Orru, H., K. L. Ebi, and B. Forsberg. 2017. "The Interplay of Climate Change and Air Pollution on Health." *Current Environmental Health Reports* 4 (4): 504–13. https://doi.org/10.1007 /s40572-017-0168-6.

WHO (World Health Organization). 2022. "Air Pollution." WHO, Geneva. https://www.who .int/health-topics/air-pollution#tab=tab_1.

World Bank. 2020. *The Global Health Cost of Ambient PM$_{2.5}$ Air Pollution*. Washington, DC: World Bank.

World Bank. Forthcoming. *Building Back a Greener Bangladesh: Country Environmental Analysis*. Washington, DC: World Bank.

Glossary

TABLE G.1 Types of air pollutants and their health effects

POLLUTANT	DESCRIPTION	HEALTH EFFECTS
Carbon monoxide (CO)	CO is a colorless, odorless gas that can be harmful when inhaled in large amounts. The greatest sources of CO to outdoor air are cars, trucks, and other vehicles or machinery that burn fossil fuels.[a]	Breathing air with a high concentration of CO reduces the amount of oxygen that can be transported in the bloodstream to critical organs like the heart and brain.[a]
Nitrogen dioxide (NO_2)	NO_2 is the main source of nitrate aerosols, which form an important fraction of $PM_{2.5}$ and, in the presence of ultraviolet light, ozone. The major sources of anthropogenic emissions of NO_2 are combustion processes: heating, power generation, and engines in vehicles and ships.	NO_2 has been linked to asthma, bronchial symptoms, lung inflammation, and reduced lung function. Bronchitis in asthmatic children increases in association with long-term exposure to NO_2.
Ozone (O_3)	Ozone is one of the major constituents of photochemical smog, formed by the reaction of sunlight with pollutants such as nitrogen oxides from vehicle and industry emissions and volatile organic compounds emitted by vehicles, solvents, and industry. The highest levels of ozone pollution occur during periods of sunny weather.	Ozone can cause breathing problems, trigger asthma, reduce lung function, and cause lung diseases.
Particulate matter (PM)	Major components of PM are sulfate, nitrates, ammonia, sodium chloride, black carbon, mineral dust, and water. They consist of a complex mixture of solid and liquid particles of organic and inorganic substances suspended in the air. Small particulate pollution has health impacts even at very low concentrations, and no threshold has been defined below which no damage to health is observed. PM numbers indicate the size of particles: $PM_{2.5}$ indicates particles of 2.5 micrometers, and PM_{10} indicates 10 micrometers.	Cardiovascular and respiratory diseases, as well as lung cancer, have been linked to PM. While PM_{10} can penetrate and lodge deep inside the lungs, $PM_{2.5}$ can penetrate the lung barrier and enter the blood system.
Sulfur dioxide (SO_2)	SO_2 is a colorless gas with a sharp odor; it is produced from the burning of fossil fuels (coal and oil) for domestic heating, power generation, and motor vehicles.	SO_2 affects the respiratory system and the functions of the lungs and causes irritation of the eyes. Inflammation of the respiratory tract causes coughing, mucus secretion, aggravation of asthma, and chronic bronchitis and makes people more prone to infections of the respiratory tract.

Source: WHO 2021.
a. Based on EPA 2022.

TABLE G.2 Bangladesh's National Limits 2005 for air pollution and the WHO Air Quality Guidelines 2021 for each pollutant

POLLUTANT	BANGLADESH'S NATIONAL LIMITS 2005	WHO AQG
Carbon monoxide (CO)	8-hour: 10 mg/m³	24-hour: 4 mg/m³
Nitrogen dioxide (NO$_2$)	Annual: 100 µg/m³	Annual: 10 µg/m³, 24-hour: 25 µg/m³
Ozone (O$_3$)	8-hour: 157 µg/m³	Peak season: 60 µg/m³, 8-hour: 100 µg/m³
Particulate matter: Fine (PM$_{2.5}$)[a]	Annual: 15 µg/m³, 24-hour: 65 µg/m³	Annual: 5 µg/m³, 24-hour: 15 µg/m³
Particulate matter: Coarse (PM$_{10}$)	Annual: 50 µg/m³, 24-hour: 150 µg/m³	Annual: 15 µg/m³, 24-hour: 45 µg/m³
Sulfur dioxide (SO$_2$)	24-hour: 365 µg/m³	24-hour: 40 µg/m³

Source: GoB 2018; WHO 2021.
Note: m³ = cubic meter; mg = milligram; µg = microgram. Annual and peak season reflect long-term exposure, while 24-hour and 8-hour reflect short-term exposure; 24-hour is the 99th percentile, that is, three to four exceedance days per year. Peak season is defined as an average of the daily maximum 8-hour mean O$_3$ concentration in the six consecutive months with the highest six-month running average O$_3$ concentration.
a. For PM$_{2.5}$, there is no "safe" threshold, because small particulate pollution has health impacts even at very low concentration levels (WHO 2021).

REFERENCES

EPA (United States Environmental Protection Agency). 2022. "Basic Information about Carbon Monoxide (CO) Outdoor Air Pollution." Updated August 2, 2022. EPA, Washington, DC.

GoB (Government of Bangladesh). 2018. *Ambient Air Quality in Bangladesh*. Dhaka: Ministry of Environment, Forest, and Climate Change. https://tinyurl.com/y93arj9y.

WHO (World Health Organization). 2020. "What Are the WHO Air Quality Guidelines?" WHO, Geneva. https://www.who.int/news-room/feature-stories/detail/what-are-the-who-air-quality-guidelines.

WHO (World Health Organization). 2021. "Ambient Air Pollution." WHO, Geneva. https://www.who.int/news-room/fact-sheets/detail/ambient-(outdoor)-air-quality-and-health.

Abbreviations

ALRI	acute lower respiratory infection
AOD	adjusted odds ratio
AQG	Air Quality Guidelines
BMRC	Bangladesh Medical Research Council
CAMS	continuous air-monitoring stations
CO	carbon monoxide
COPD	chronic obstructive pulmonary disease
COVID-19	coronavirus disease
DCC	Dhaka City Corporation
DoE	Department of Environment
ED	emergency department
GDP	gross domestic product
HPV	human papillomavirus
IARC	International Agency for Research on Cancer
IEDCR	Institute of Epidemiology and Disease Control Research
IQR	interquartile range
LDL	low-density lipoprotein
NCD	noncommunicable disease
NO_2	nitrogen dioxide
O_3	ozone
OAR	odds-adjusted ratio
PM	particulate matter
$PM_{2.5}$	fine particulate matter
PM_{10}	coarse particulate matter
POI	point of interest
ppb	parts per billion
PSU	primary sampling unit
SO_2	sulfur dioxide
VOC	volatile organic compound
WaSH	water, sanitation, and hygiene
WHO	World Health Organization
WHO-5	World Health Organization Well-Being Index
$\mu g/m^3$	micrograms per cubic meter

1 Background and Context

AIR POLLUTION, BANGLADESH'S VULNERABILITY, AND OBJECTIVES

Air pollution is a major cause of premature death and disease globally and is the world's largest environmental risk to health (India State-Level Disease Burden Initiative Air Pollution Collaborators 2020). The World Health Organization defines air pollution as the contamination of the indoor or outdoor environment by any chemical, physical, or biological agent that modifies the natural characteristics of the atmosphere (WHO n.d.). In 2019, air pollution was the world's fourth-leading risk factor for early deaths and caused an estimated 6.67 million deaths globally (HEI 2020). Exposure to ambient or outdoor air pollution results in morbidity and mortality from diseases such as chronic obstructive pulmonary disease (COPD), ischemic heart disease, lung cancer, pneumonia, and stroke. Most deaths attributed to air pollution are caused by inhalation of fine particulate matter with a diameter of 2.5 micrometers ($PM_{2.5}$) (World Bank 2020).

Almost 99 percent of the global population breathes air containing high levels of pollutants that exceed the safe limits set by WHO. Low- and middle-income countries suffer more than better-off countries, with exposure levels that are significantly higher (WHO n.d.). Health damages caused by air pollution are substantial—around 4.1 million deaths and 15 billion days of illness in 2016. This translates into an estimated welfare cost of approximately US$5.7 trillion, equivalent to 4.8 percent of global gross domestic product (GDP) (World Bank 2020).

Between 2018 and 2021, Bangladesh was ranked as the most polluted country in the world and Dhaka as the second most polluted city over the same duration (measured using annual average $PM_{2.5}$ concentration weighted by population) (IQAir 2021). Consequently, the effect on human health is deleterious; exposure to ambient $PM_{2.5}$ caused an estimated 78,145–88,229 deaths in Bangladesh in 2019 and between 220,000 and 248,000 disability-adjusted life years lived with illness, corresponding to 1.0–1.1 billion days lived with illness (World Bank, forthcoming a). The annual cost of these health effects translates to losses of between US$11.5 billion and US$13 billion in 2019, equivalent to 3.9 to 4.4 percent of Bangladesh's GDP that year. A third of the estimated deaths caused by exposure to ambient $PM_{2.5}$ were in the Dhaka division, the most polluted part of the country. Four of the top five causes leading to deaths between 2009 and 2019 in Bangladesh were directly associated with air pollution: chronic obstructive pulmonary disease, ischemic heart disease, stroke, and lower respiratory tract infection (figure 1.1). Moreover, air pollution remained the second-strongest risk factor leading to deaths and disability in Bangladesh between 2009 and 2019 (figure 1.2). Approximately 31,300 more deaths were attributed to $PM_{2.5}$ in 2019 than in 2010 (HEI 2020).

The overall objective of this report is to identify the short-term effects of ambient air pollution on human health in Bangladesh using a combination of household data primarily on individual health conditions, localized data on air pollution levels, and analysis of existing literature. Given the varying sources of air pollution, the data collection sites included Dhaka (as the primary location) and Sylhet (as the comparator) during the dry season (between January and February 2022). The recommendations contained are based on the evidence generated through this report and contextualized for strengthening the health systems to be better prepared to deal with air-pollution-related mortality and morbidity. The findings and recommendations are expected to assist practitioners and subject matter experts in policy dialogue under the overall framework of the government's *Mujib Climate Prosperity Plan Decade 2030*. At the same time, the report will contribute to advancing the World Bank's corporate mandate relating to climate change.

FIGURE 1.1

Top 10 causes of total number of deaths in 2019 and percent change 2000–2019, all ages combined

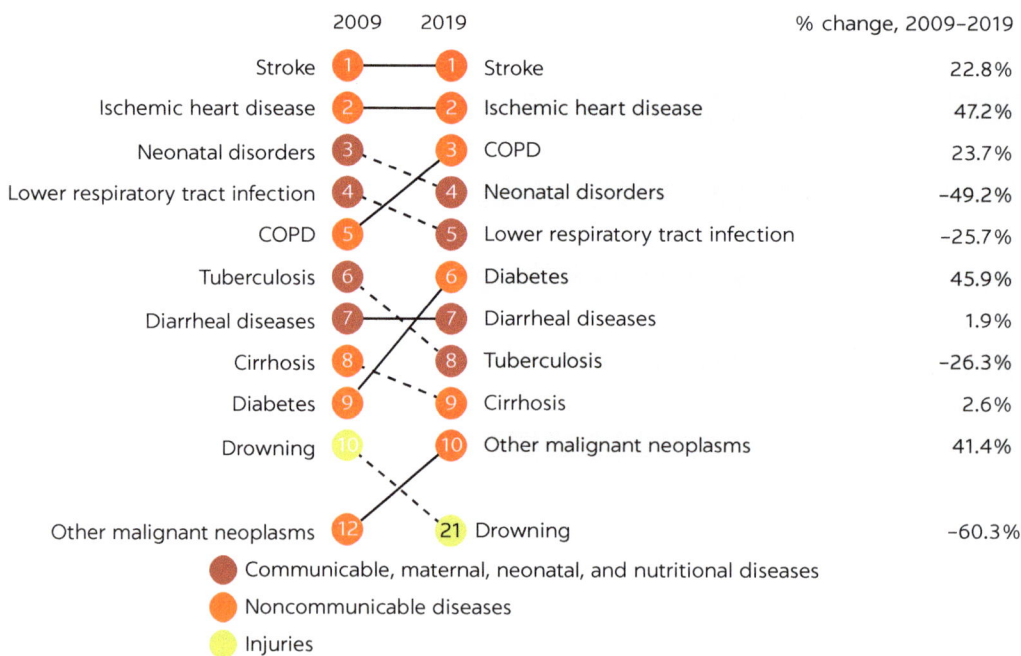

2009	2019	% change, 2009–2019
Stroke (1)	(1) Stroke	22.8%
Ischemic heart disease (2)	(2) Ischemic heart disease	47.2%
Neonatal disorders (3)	(3) COPD	23.7%
Lower respiratory tract infection (4)	(4) Neonatal disorders	−49.2%
COPD (5)	(5) Lower respiratory tract infection	−25.7%
Tuberculosis (6)	(6) Diabetes	45.9%
Diarrheal diseases (7)	(7) Diarrheal diseases	1.9%
Cirrhosis (8)	(8) Tuberculosis	−26.3%
Diabetes (9)	(9) Cirrhosis	2.6%
Drowning (10)	(10) Other malignant neoplasms	41.4%
Other malignant neoplasms (12)	(21) Drowning	−60.3%

● Communicable, maternal, neonatal, and nutritional diseases
● Noncommunicable diseases
● Injuries

Source: IHME 2019.
Note: COPD = chronic obstructive pulmonary disease.

FIGURE 1.2

Top 10 risks contributing to total number of disability-adjusted life years in 2019 and percent change 2000–2019, all ages combined

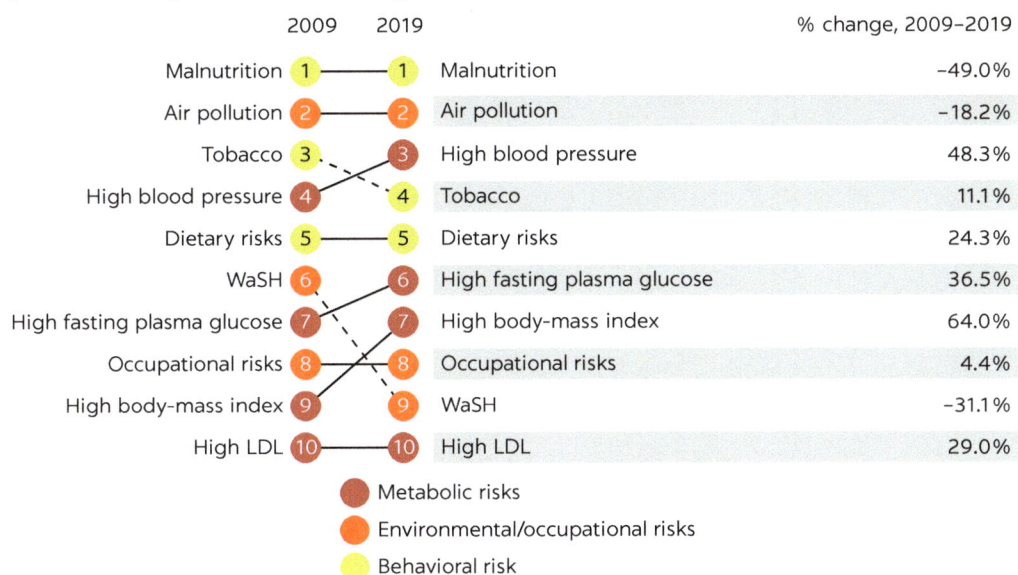

	2009	2019		% change, 2009–2019
Malnutrition	1	1	Malnutrition	−49.0%
Air pollution	2	2	Air pollution	−18.2%
Tobacco	3	3	High blood pressure	48.3%
High blood pressure	4	4	Tobacco	11.1%
Dietary risks	5	5	Dietary risks	24.3%
WaSH	6	6	High fasting plasma glucose	36.5%
High fasting plasma glucose	7	7	High body-mass index	64.0%
Occupational risks	8	8	Occupational risks	4.4%
High body-mass index	9	9	WaSH	−31.1%
High LDL	10	10	High LDL	29.0%

Metabolic risks
Environmental/occupational risks
Behavioral risk

Source: IHME 2019.
Note: LDL = low-density lipoprotein cholesterol; WaSH = water, sanitation, and hygiene.

HISTORICAL TRENDS OF AMBIENT AIR POLLUTION IN BANGLADESH

This section explores the trends in ambient air pollution ($PM_{2.5}$) in Bangladesh between 2013 and 2021 using data collected through continuous air monitoring stations (CAMS) by the Department of Environment (DOE), Ministry of Environment and Forestry, government of Bangladesh. The analysis focuses on data from Dhaka and Sylhet, the two areas surveyed as part of this report. The findings presented are generalized trends, and more localized information is needed to understand these patterns better.

The CAMS data suggest that Dhaka was the most polluted division in Bangladesh between 2013 and 2021—with an average $PM_{2.5}$ concentration of 87 micrograms per cubic meter ($\mu g/m^3$)—while Sylhet was the least polluted, with an average $PM_{2.5}$ concentration of 46 $\mu g/m^3$. The western divisions, comprising Khulna and Rajshahi (average $PM_{2.5}$ concentrations of 65 $\mu g/m^3$ and 66 $\mu g/m^3$, respectively), were more polluted than the eastern ones of Sylhet and Chattogram (average $PM_{2.5}$ concentrations of 61 $\mu g/m^3$ and 46 $\mu g/m^3$, respectively) over the same period. Barisal was the second most polluted division after Dhaka with an average $PM_{2.5}$ concentration level of 73 $\mu g/m^3$ between 2003 and 2021. Map 1.1 provides a graphical overview of the pollution levels across the country.

Notably, although national manufacturing and industrial activities are more concentrated in the eastern divisions of the country while the western is more agriculturally intensive, air pollution levels are higher in the west than the east. This may be explained, at least to some extent, by transboundary air pollution as suggested by findings from Begum et al. (2014). Estimates indicate that 40 percent of total $PM_{2.5}$ concentration in Khulna originates from outside of the country, for example (World Bank, forthcoming b).

MAP 1.1

PM$_{2.5}$ average annual concentration levels (micrograms per cubic meter), 2013–2021

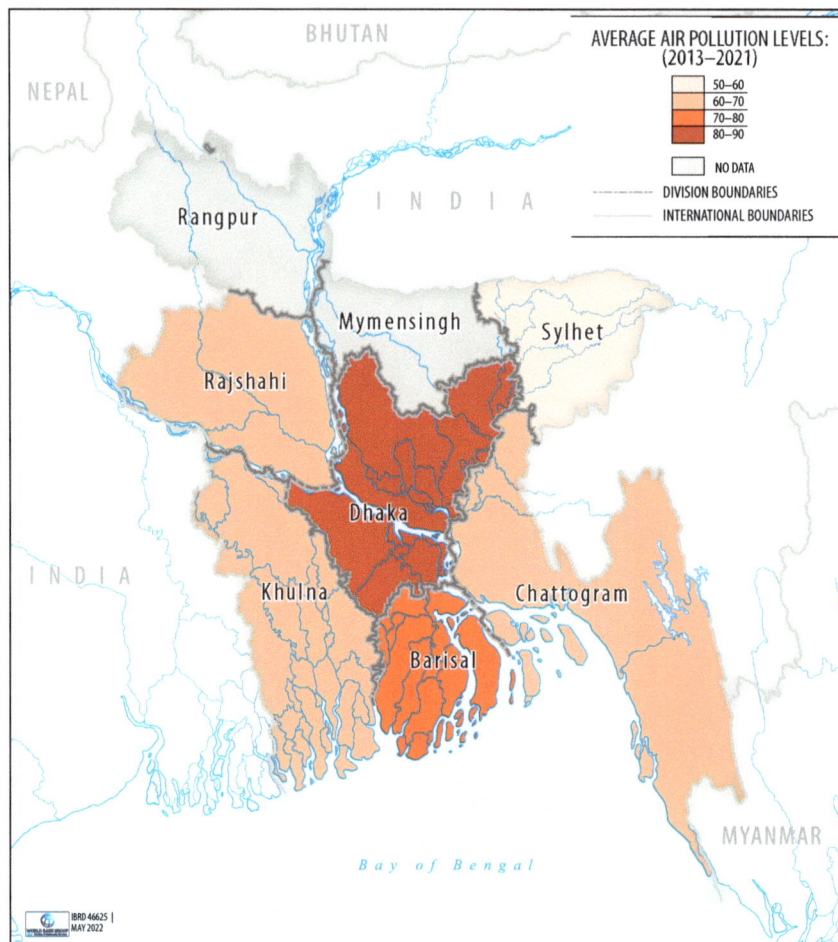

Source: Original figure for this publication.
Note: PM$_{2.5}$ = fine particulate matter with a diameter of 2.5 micrometers.

Comparison of trends in air pollution levels by the administrative divisions are illustrated in map 1.2. Sylhet, Chattogram, and Barisal divisions were less polluted in 2021 compared to 2013 (as measured by exposure to PM$_{2.5}$), while the levels increased for Dhaka, Khulna, and Rajshahi divisions. For Mymensingh and Rangpur divisions, data for 2013 were not available, as the CAMS were set up in 2018–2019.

Analysis of annual trends in PM$_{2.5}$ exposure levels for Dhaka and Sylhet divisions suggests that pollution levels have been intensifying in Dhaka while decreasing in Sylhet between 2003 and 2021. Figure 1.3 shows annualized observations of PM$_{2.5}$ levels and linear trends in its exposure over time.

For Dhaka, the major sectors contributing to air pollution are the small industries (including brick kilns) and residential. Equally important are the source of air pollution that varies considerably, with the main sources being outside of Dhaka division and transborder pollution. Estimates indicate that 20 percent of total PM$_{2.5}$ concentration in Dhaka originates from outside of the country (World Bank, forthcoming b).

MAP 1.2

Average annual PM$_{2.5}$ concentration levels (micrograms per cubic meter)

a. 2013

b. 2021

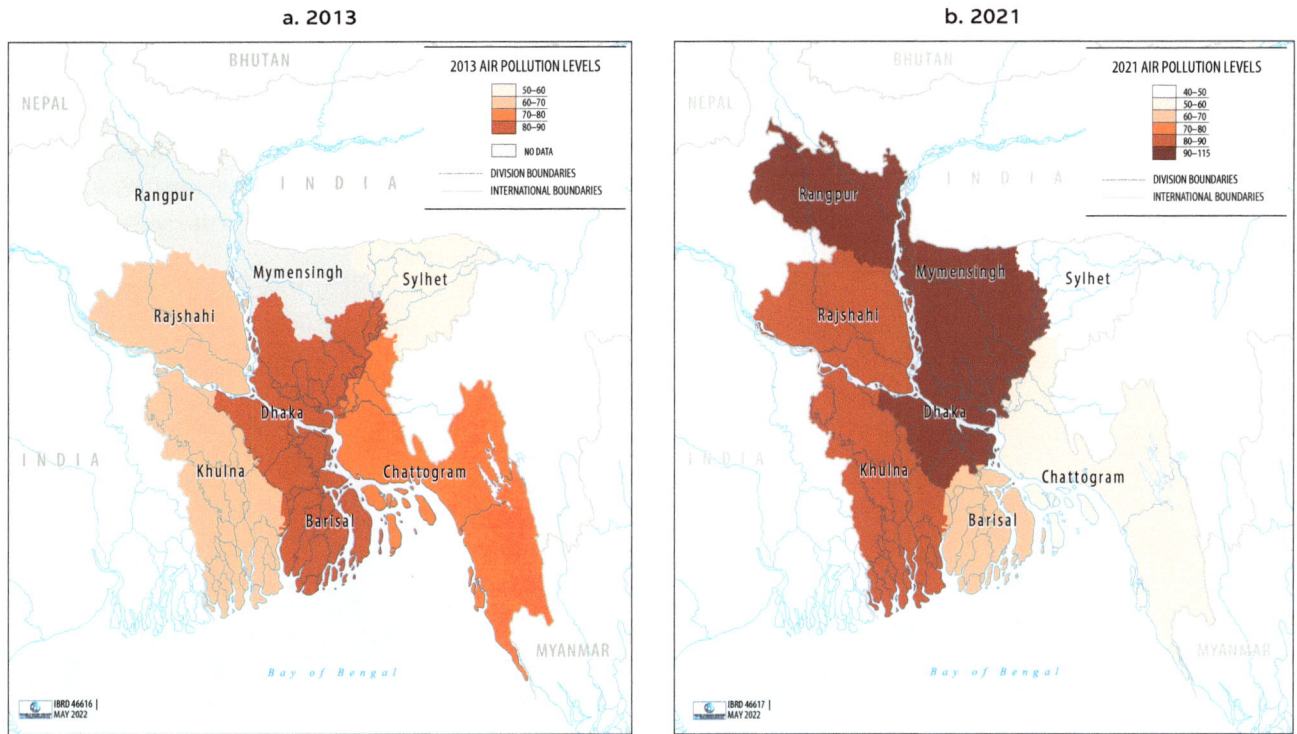

Source: Original figure for this publication.
Note: PM$_{2.5}$ = fine particulate matter with a diameter of 2.5 micrometers.

FIGURE 1.3

PM$_{2.5}$ annual average concentration levels for Dhaka and Sylhet, 2013–2021

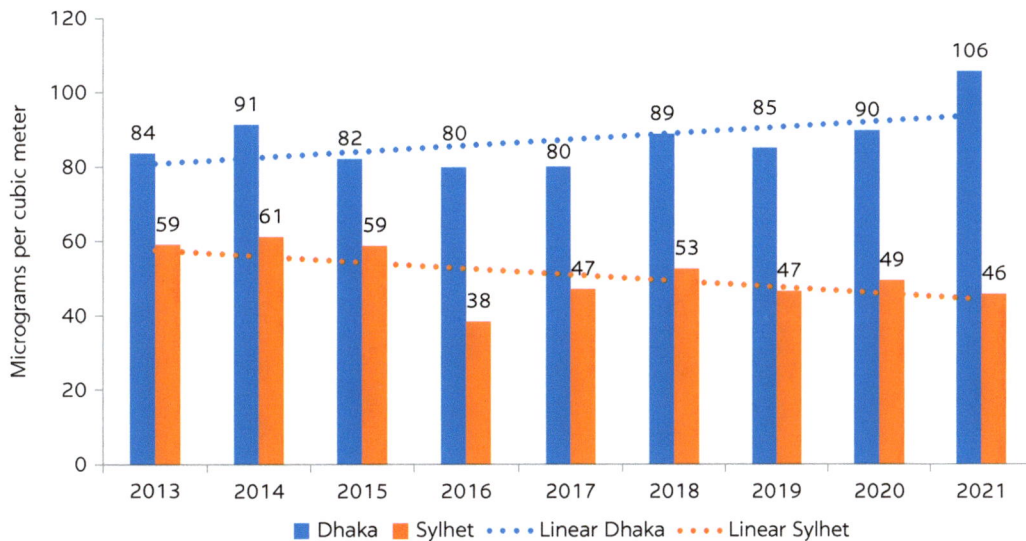

Source: Original figure for this publication.
Note: PM$_{2.5}$ = fine particulate matter with a diameter of 2.5 micrometers.

PATHWAYS OF AIR POLLUTION'S IMPACT ON HEALTH

There are at least six air pollutants of major public health concern identified by WHO, which include fine particulate matter ($PM_{2.5}$), coarse particulate matter (PM_{10}), ozone at ground level (O_3, not the ozone layer in the upper atmosphere), nitrogen dioxide (NO_2), sulfur dioxide (SO_2), and carbon monoxide (CO). Particulate matter, a mixture of solid particles and liquid droplets found in the air, is a common proxy indicator for air pollution. $PM_{2.5}$ are particles with a diameter of 2.5 microns or less and PM_{10} are particles with a diameter of 10 microns or less (World Bank 2020). For comparison, human hair measures between 50 to 180 microns in diameter, a salt grain measures 70 microns, and fine beach sand measures 90 microns (figure 1.4) (IQAir 2021). The human nose is able to filter most of the coarse particles, but the fine ($PM_{2.5}$) and ultrafine (PM_1) particles enter the lungs and can even be absorbed into the blood, causing considerable risk to human health.

$PM_{2.5}$ is considered the most harmful for human health as it causes multiple health issues and is most prevalent in the air (IQAir 2021). Due to its microscopic size, $PM_{2.5}$ can, as mentioned, enter the bloodstream through the lungs, affecting all major organs. Exposure to $PM_{2.5}$ can lead to both short- and long-term diseases in the cardiovascular and respiratory systems and exacerbate preexisting conditions such as asthma and lung cancer, among others. Exposure to $PM_{2.5}$ can be particularly detrimental for children, with consequences ranging from low birth weight and developmental delay at age three, to psychological and behavioral problems later in life, including symptoms of attention deficit hyperactivity disorder, anxiety, and depression (WHO 2021). The other air pollutants, such as NO_2 and SO_2, cause diseases related to the cardiovascular and respiratory system causing cough and mucus secretion, worsening

FIGURE 1.4
Relative sizes of particulate matter

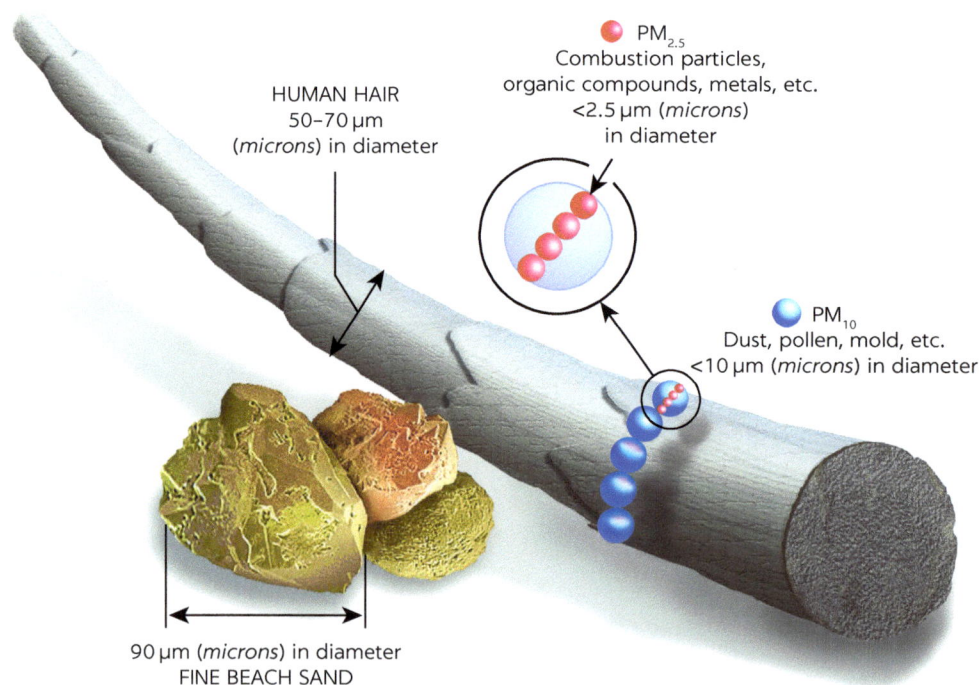

Source: US Environmental Protection Agency (2022), https://www.epa.gov/pm-pollution/particulate-matter-pm-basics.

TABLE 1.1 Diseases linked to air pollution, by organ system

Brain	Stroke, dementia, Parkinson's disease
Eye	Conjunctivitis, dry eye disease, blepharitis, cataracts
Heart	Ischemic heart disease, hypertension, congestive heart failure, arrhythmias
Lung	Chronic obstructive pulmonary disease, asthma, lung cancer, chronic laryngitis, acute and chronic bronchitis
Liver	Hepatic steatosis, hepatocellular carcinoma
Pancreas	Type 1 and 2 diabetes
Gastrointestinal	Gastric cancer, colorectal cancer, inflammatory bowel disease, Crohn's disease, appendicitis
Urogenital	Bladder cancer, kidney cancer, prostate hyperplasia
Joints	Rheumatic diseases
Bone	Osteoporosis, fractures
Nose	Allergic rhinitis
Skin	Atopic skin disease, skin aging, urticaria, dermographism, seborrhea, acne

Source: Schraufnagel et al. 2019.

asthma and chronic bronchitis, and making people more susceptible to respiratory tract infections. As air pollution affects the respiratory and cardiovascular systems over time, it can make people more vulnerable to COVID-19 (HEI 2020). For instance, a study conducted in the United States found that mortality from COVID-19 infection increased by 11 percent for every 1 microgram per cubic meter increase in air pollution (measured using exposure to $PM_{2.5}$) (Wu et al. 2020).

The glossary provides an overview of the types of air pollutants, their major health impacts, and the safe exposure limits set by the government of Bangladesh in 2005 and the WHO (2021) air quality guidelines. Table 1.1 presents an overview of organ systems that are affected by air pollution. Appendix A provides a detailed review of existing literature assessing the effect of air pollution on health.

THE CLIMATE CHANGE AND AIR POLLUTION NEXUS

Air pollution causes the climate to change, while climate change worsens the quality of breathable air (UCAR 2022). This is mainly due to the emission of greenhouse gases such as CO_2, O_3, and particulate matter from the burning of fossil fuels. Due to global warming, extreme weather conditions such as heat waves and drought are more frequent, which can adversely affect air quality. In addition, burning fossil fuels and other unclean energy sources causes increased levels of particulate matter and other pollutants in the air. Air pollutants and climate variables (temperature, surface pressure, and relative humidity) interact and contribute to climate change. In densely populated regions, climate change is expected to significantly exacerbate air pollution (Orru, Ebi, and Forsberg 2017). In several urbanized areas of the world, air pollution patterns are evolving due to climate change and other factors, with a significant impact on respiratory health. For example, studies from Europe on heatwave episodes have consistently shown a synergistic effect of air pollution and high temperatures (Sario 2013). Based on existing literature, the conceptual framework for these interactions is summarized in figure 1.5.

FIGURE 1.5

Climate change and air pollution nexus: a theoretical framework

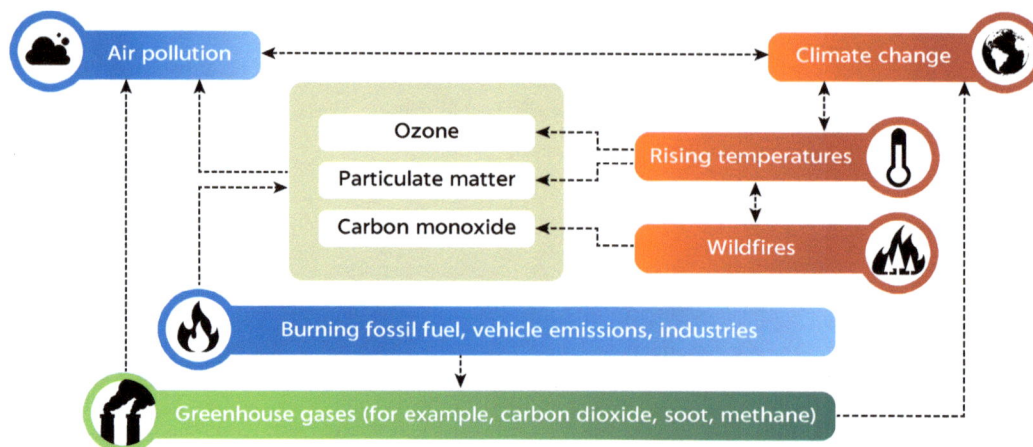

Source: Original compilation from authors for this publication.

APPROVAL PROCESSES

Approval from the Bangladesh Medical Research Council (BMRC) was obtained prior to commencement of the survey. All ethical protocols and standards of BMRC were adhered to during fieldwork. The following procedures were followed:

- Written informed consent of the interviewees was obtained.
- Names of respondents were not recorded; instead, a unique identity number was attached to the household. The privacy of information collected was ensured by keeping it anonymous (not attaching names of the respondents to the data).
- Data on nationality and religion were not collected.
- Respondents' personal information was not included in data files.
- Results were presented in aggregate form, without identifying any individual.

The draft report was shared with the Institute of Epidemiology and Disease Control Research (IEDCR) of the Ministry of Health and Family Welfare and the Department of Environment of the Ministry of Environment, Forestry, and Climate Change of the government of Bangladesh before finalization. For quality assurance, the report was reviewed at an internal World Bank meeting, chaired by Dandan Chen, Acting Country Director for Bangladesh and Bhutan. The review was organized to discuss the methodology, findings, and the potential implications of the conclusions and recommendations for Bangladesh. Based on detailed discussions during the internal review and extensive comments provided by the reviewers, the report was finalized. Reviewers included the following World Bank experts: Stephen Geoffrey Dorey (Health Specialist), Jostein Nygard (Senior Environmental Specialist), and Muthukumara Mani (Lead Economist), as well as Iqbal Ahmed (Senior Environmental Specialist), M. Khaliquzzaman (Senior Environmental Consultant), and Ana Luisa Gomes Lima (Senior Environmental Specialist).

REFERENCES

Begum, B.A., Md. Nasiruddin, Scott Randall, Bjarne Sivertsen, and Philip K. Hopke. 2014. "Identification and Apportionment of Sources from Air Particulate Matter at Urban Environments in Bangladesh." *Current Journal of Applied Science and Technology* 4 (27): 3930–55. http://doi.org/0.9734/BJAST/2014/11247.

HEI (Health Effects Institute). 2020. *State of Global Air 2020: Special Report*. Boston, MA: Health Effects Institute.

IHME (Institute for Health Metrics and Evaluation). 2019. "Bangladesh." Seattle: University of Washington. https://www.healthdata.org/bangladesh.

India State-Level Disease Burden Initiative Air Pollution Collaborators. 2020. "Health and Economic Impact of Air Pollution in the States of India: The Global Burden of Disease Study 2019." *Lancet Planetary Health* 5 (1; January 2021): e25–38. http://doi.org/10.1016/S2542 -5196(20)30298-9.

IQAir. 2021. *World Air Quality Report: Region and City PM2.5 Ranking*. Goldach: Switzerland. https://www.iqair.com/bangladesh/dhaka.

Orru, H., K. L. Ebi, and B. Forsberg. 2017. "The Interplay of Climate Change and Air Pollution on Health." *Current Environmental Health Reports* 4 (4): 504–13. http://doi.org/10.1007 /s40572-017-0168-6.

Sario, M. D. 2013. "Climate Change, Extreme Weather Events, Air Pollution and Respiratory Health in Europe." *European Respiratory Journal* 42: 826–43. https://doi.org/10.1183 /09031936.00074712.

Schraufnagel, Dean E., John R. Balmes, Clayton T. Cowl, Sara De Matteis, Soon-Hee Jung, Kevin Mortimer, Rogelio Perez-Padilla, et al. 2019. "Air Pollution and Noncommunicable Diseases: A Review by the Forum of International Respiratory Societies' Environmental Committee," part 2: "Air Pollution and Organ Systems." *Chest* 155 (2): 417–426. https://doi.org/10.1016 /j.chest.2018.10.041.

UCAR (University Corporation for Atmospheric Research Center for Science Education). 2022. "Air Quality and Climate Change." Boulder, CO: UCAR. https://scied.ucar.edu/learning-zone /air-quality/air-quality-and-climate-change.

WHO (World Health Organization). 2021. "WHO Global Air Quality Guidelines." Geneva: WHO. https://www.who.int/news-room/questions-and-answers/item/who-global -air-quality-guidelines.

WHO (World Health Organization). n.d. "Air Pollution." Geneva: WHO (accessed October 5, 2019). http://www.who.int/airpollution/en/.

World Bank. 2020. *The Global Health Cost of Ambient PM$_{2.5}$ Air Pollution*. Washington, DC: World Bank.

World Bank. Forthcoming a. *Building Back a Greener Bangladesh: Country Environmental Analysis*. Washington, DC: World Bank.

World Bank. Forthcoming b. *Toward Clean Air: Air Pollution and Public Health in South Asia*. Washington, DC: World Bank.

Wu, X., R. C. Nethery, M. B. Sabath, D. Braun, and F. Dominici. 2020. "Air Pollution and COVID-19 Mortality in the United States: Strengths and Limitations of an Ecological Regression Analysis." *Science Advances* 6 (45). https://doi.org/10.1126/sciadv.abd4049.

2 Data, Methods, and Respondent Profile

DATA AND METHODS

The survey for this study was implemented between January and February 2022, when the country experiences the highest levels of air pollution. The survey canvassed 12,250 individuals from 2,500 households, stratified across four sites reflecting the varying sources and levels of pollution: (1) persistent traffic,[1] (2) major construction[2] and persistent traffic, (3) brick kilns, and (4) comparator sites, across 100 primary sampling units (PSUs). Based on reported findings from Bangladesh's Department of Environment (GoB 2018), the first two sites are located in the North and South Dhaka City Corporations (DCCs), while the brick kilns are located in the outskirts of the DCC area—these together represent the most polluted part of the country, as mentioned in chapter 1. The comparator is rural Sylhet, selected because it is one of the least polluted locations in the country (GoB 2018). Map 2.1 shows the locations of the PSUs across the sites. Areas in the outskirts of Dhaka covering brick kilns also include other factories and industries as well as the Siddhirganj power plant. Because the main source of air pollution in these areas is the brick kilns, the site has been named accordingly.

The sampling was designed to capture the range of varying pollution exposures and associated morbidities across each of the study sites.[3] The selection of the PSUs was driven by the presence of points of interest (POIs) for each location. Adjacent PSUs are located at least 0.75 kilometers apart to minimize cross-PSU contamination of pollutants to the extent possible. In each PSU, a listing exercise was carried out within a 0.25-kilometer radius of the POI to identify potential households to be included in the survey. The final list of 25 households from each PSU (25 PSUs per each of the study areas) were randomly selected based on stratification criteria set a priori.[4] Appendix B, table B.1 shows the distribution of the sample.

MAP 2.1

Primary sampling unit locations

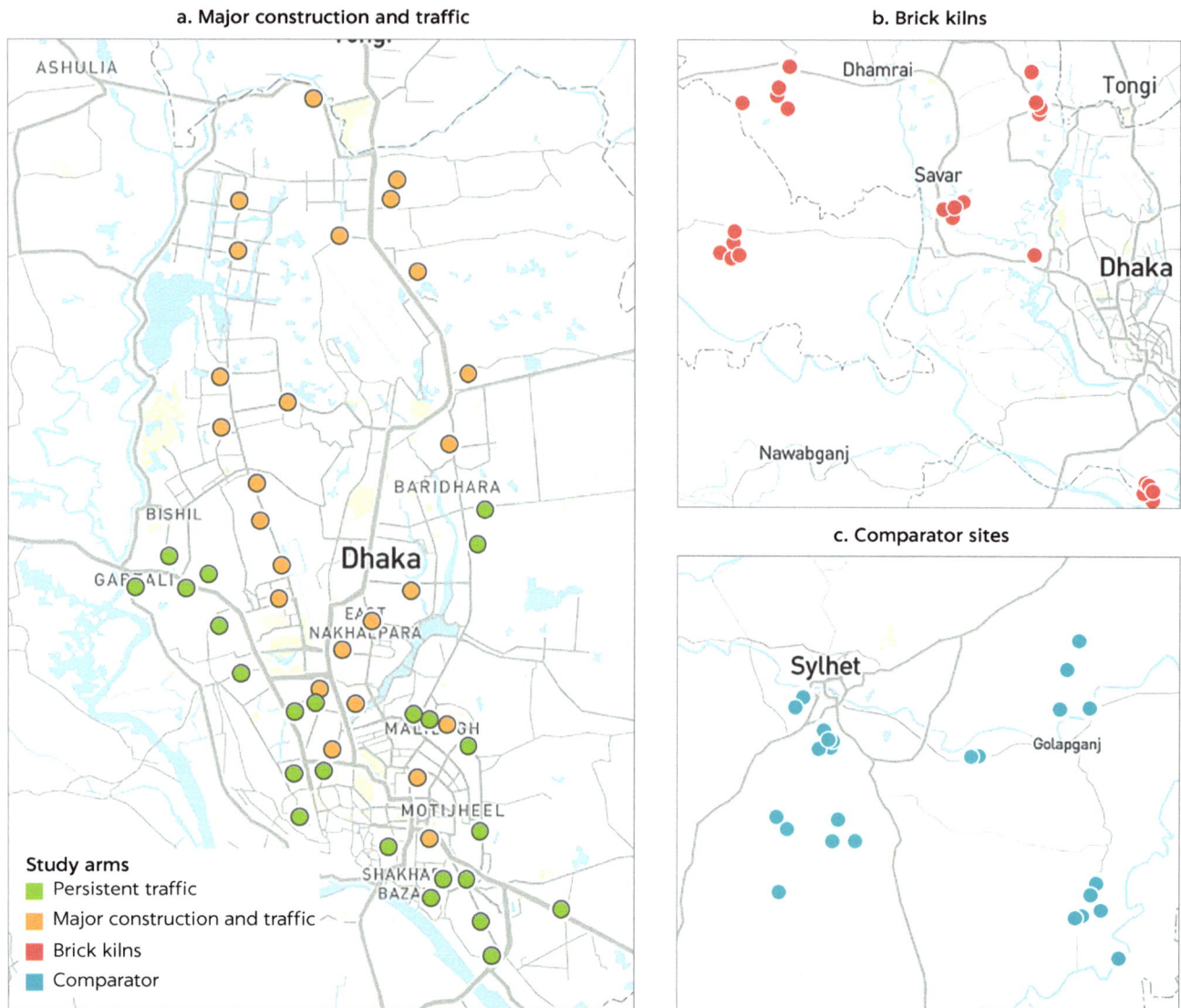

a. Major construction and traffic

b. Brick kilns

c. Comparator sites

Study arms
- Persistent traffic
- Major construction and traffic
- Brick kilns
- Comparator

Source: Original maps for this publication.
Note: Figure shows the distribution of the primary sampling units by study sites.

The structured questionnaire administered during the survey comprised both individual- and household-level questions. Individual-level questions were directed at each member of the household. For members below 10 years of age, the mother or primary caregiver furnished the requisite information. The primary female member of the household responded to household-level questions. Individual-level information revolved primarily around the household members' physical and mental health conditions that are typically associated with exposure to air pollution, socioeconomic outcomes, time spent indoors and outdoors, and related factors. The household-level information includes a relative wealth index as well as the source of energy for cooking. Further details on information collected are presented in appendix C.

Personal air-quality measuring devices[5] were used to collect ambient and household pollution conditions (Jauvion et al. 2020). The devices produce reading for several pollutants: (1) particulate matter (PM) 1, (2) $PM_{2.5}$, (3) PM_{10}, (4) nitrogen dioxide, and (5) volatile organic compounds. For ambient air pollution, typically in a central location within each PSU, air quality was measured between 09:00 and 11:00 hours and once more between 19:00 and 21:00 hours for two days: a day before and on the day of the survey, with the assumption that the ambient weather conditions remain comparable over the two days. The average of all four readings is used to calculate the final exposure to ambient air pollution. The same strategy was used to measure indoor conditions for each of the households, typically in a central room.[6] The final figures used for analysis are the average of ambient-outdoor and household-indoor air pollution levels, weighted by the amount of time spent indoors or outdoors.

Based on the existing literature and WHO's 2021 Air Quality Guidelines (AQG) (WHO 2021), the study focuses on the $PM_{2.5}$ and PM_{10} for all subsequent analysis. To normalize the exposure levels and facilitate a more intuitive understanding, the air pollutants are expressed as the percentage above (or below) the WHO's 2021 AQG 2021.[7] A binary logistic model was used to establish correlations between physical and mental health outcomes among the respondents, as well as for the analyses of heterogeneity across the four study sites. A detailed explanation of the methods, including results interpretation, are furnished in appendix C.

RESPONDENT PROFILE

This section delineates the underlying demographic and socioeconomic characteristics of the respondent pool. Figure 2.1 shows the demographic characteristics of the sample. Approximately 51 and 49 percent of the sample are represented by women and men, respectively. Elderly people older than 65 years, followed by children between 0 and 5 years, represent the smallest proportion of the study population. The largest proportion are represented by those 16 to 35 years of age. Approximately 46 percent of the respondents are married. About 39.9 percent of the respondents above the age of 5 report never attending any formal schooling, while less than 1 in 10 (8.8 percent) have completed high school education or more.

Figure 2.2 presents the activity status of respondents above 5 years of age, across each of the study sites. Around 17.8 percent of all respondents are engaged in low-skilled outdoor wage work, as day laborers, porters, and other workers at the time of the survey. The proportion of individuals engaged in low-skilled indoor work is 7 percent overall. Approximately 15.1 percent of the respondents in the sample are engaged in indoor skilled wage activities. Nearly a third of the sample (31.3 percent) are homemakers.

Socioeconomic status using relative wealth index quintiles is presented in figure 2.3. Of the 18.7 percent of the sample in the poorest quintile, the largest proportion live in areas with major construction and persistent traffic, followed by those with persistent traffic. While the trends among those in the mid quintiles (poor, mid, and rich) are mixed, the richest among the sample are from the comparator site, followed by those living in areas with brick kilns.

FIGURE 2.1

Demographic distribution of the sample

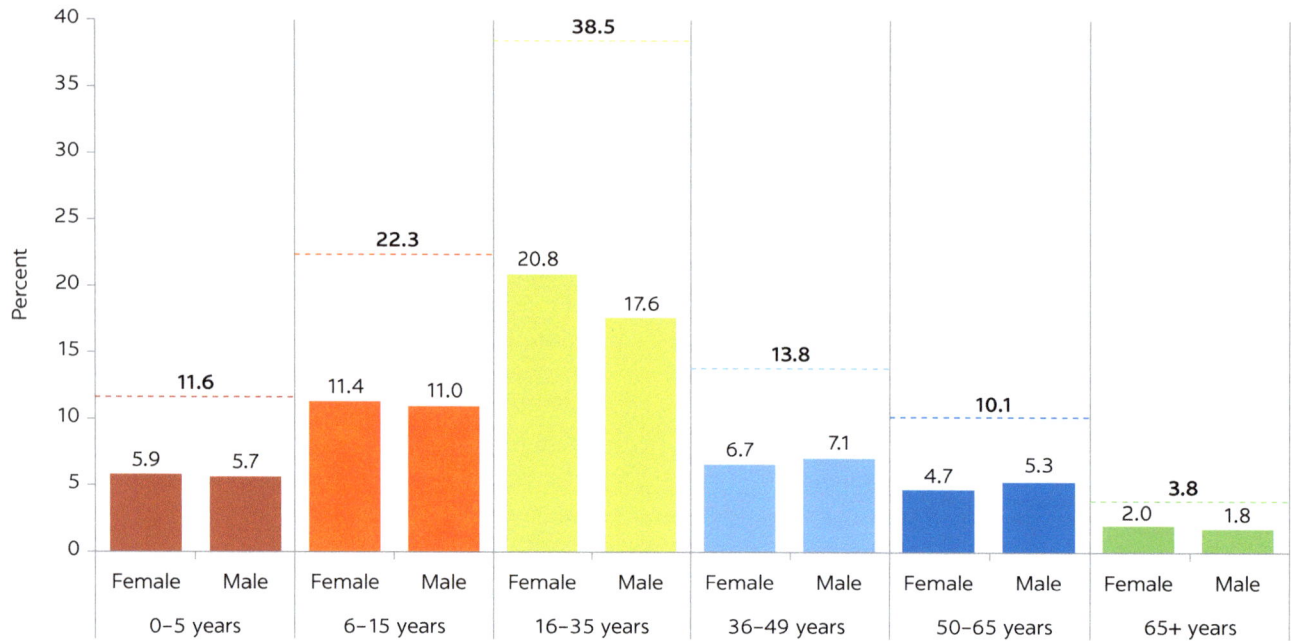

Source: Based on original calculations for this publication.
Note: Dotted lines represent the aggregated sample mean for each age group.

FIGURE 2.2

Activity status of respondents, by study site

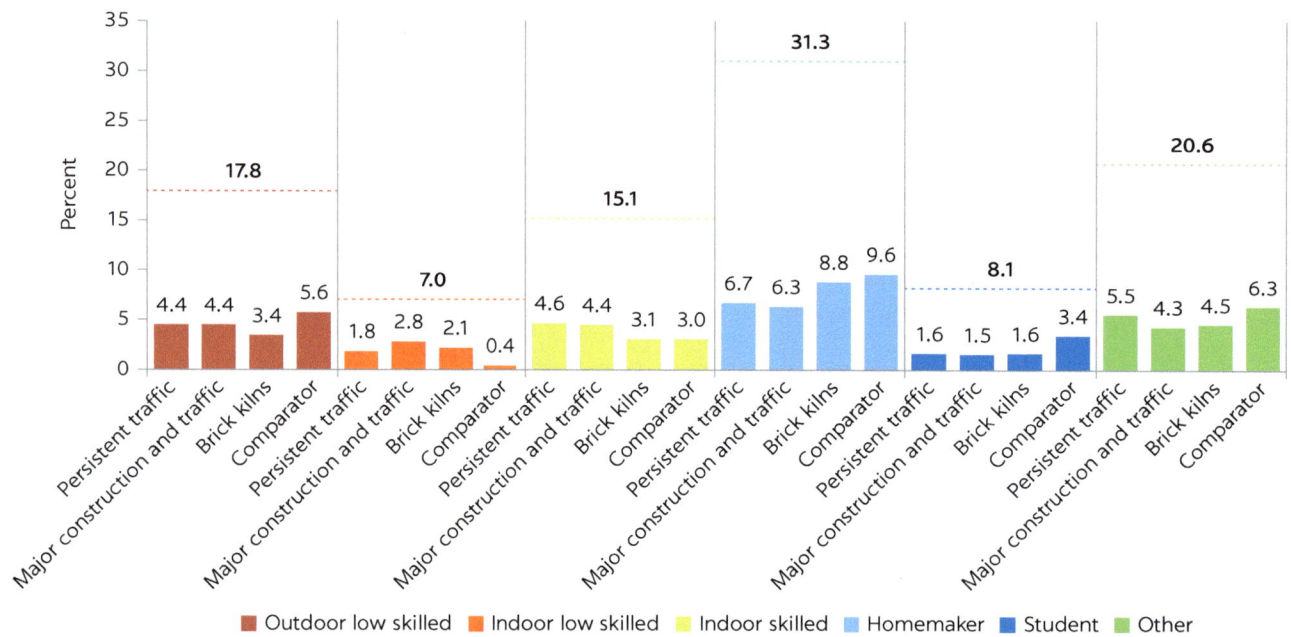

Source: Based on original calculations for this publication.
Note: Dotted lines represent the aggregated sample mean for each activity. For this categorization, individuals above 5 years have been used. The surveyed households were stratified across four sites reflecting the varying sources and levels of pollution: (1) persistent traffic in the North and South Dhaka City Corporation areas, (2) major construction and persistent traffic in North and South Dhaka City Corporation areas, (3) brick kilns in the outskirts of Dhaka city, and (4) comparator site in rural Sylhet, given that it is one of the least polluted locations in the country.

FIGURE 2.3

Relative wealth status of respondents, by study site

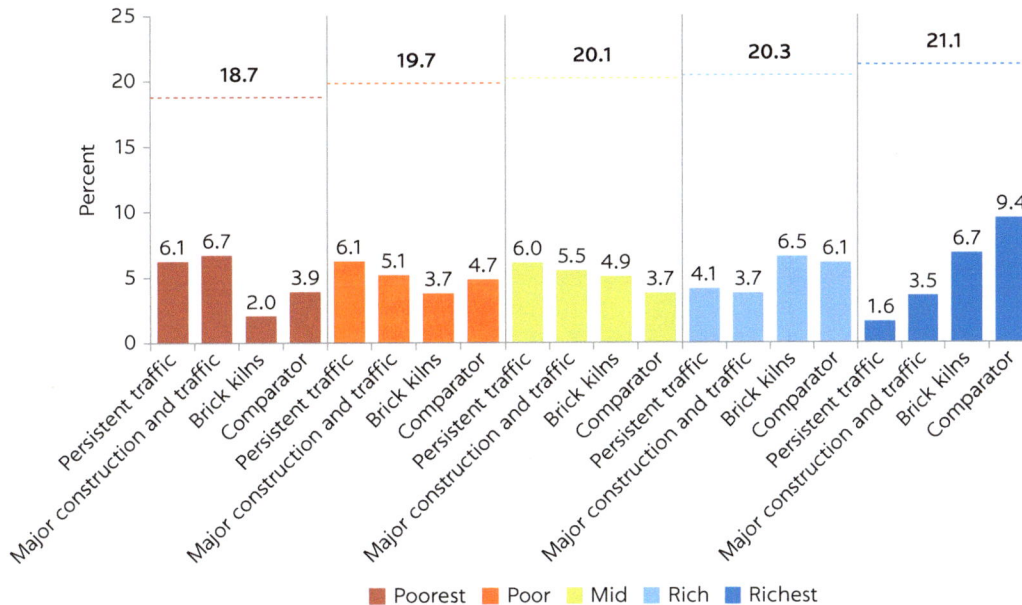

Source: Based on original calculations for this publication.
Note: Dotted lines represent the aggregated sample mean for each wealth quintile. The surveyed households were stratified across four sites reflecting the varying levels of pollution: (1) persistent traffic in the North and South Dhaka City Corporation areas, (2) major construction and persistent traffic in North and South Dhaka City Corporation areas, (3) brick kilns in the outskirts of Dhaka city, and (4) comparator site in rural Sylhet, given that it is one of the least polluted locations in the country.

STUDY LIMITATIONS

This is the first study of its kind, in which localized pollution levels (at the PSU and household levels) are measured using personal air quality measurement devices and, as such, merits further validation of the readings in the current setting. The study attempts to mimic a 24-hour exposure level using data collected twice per day (in the morning and evening) over a two-day period—the findings will therefore not be directly comparable to a true 24-hour estimate. However, as the study uniformly deploys the data collection strategy, both in terms of timing and duration of the readings, any potential biases will be universally applied across all locations, thereby providing relative readings of the levels of exposure to pollutants. At the individual level, the study is unable to account for exposure to second-hand smoke or conditions the individuals experience when in inaccessible locations such as the workplace. However, the study does account for time-use during the day to collect information on the number of hours individuals spend outdoors (such as in the streets, on balconies, or other open locations); indoors without air-conditioning (as represented by homes or shops); and locations with air-conditioning or heating, ventilation, and air-conditioning systems (such as in homes, offices, or vehicles) to reach an approximate weighted measure. For historical analyses of air pollution levels, data from the Department of Environment have been used, based on the 11 continuous air-monitoring stations spread across the country. (Two additional stations were installed as recently as 2019/20. See appendix B, map B1.). The historical analysis is thus at best an indication of observed patterns.

NOTES

1. Persistent traffic refers to large arterial roads that are known to be perennially congested with traffic.
2. Major construction refers to large city-level infrastructural development projects such as elevated expressways and the metrorail network construction taking place in the Dhaka City Corporations.
3. For an ex post power calculation of the minimum effect size that can be captured by this sample, the study assessed the incidences of self-reported respiratory illnesses as an individual-level health outcome. For the control group, the mean of this binary variable is 0.17, with an intracluster correlation across the PSUs of 0.01. The average number of individuals for whom this data is collected is 137 per enumeration area. Based on these parameters, the minimum detectable effect for this outcome is 0.041 at 80 percent power.
4. In line with the guidelines set a priori, the sample households were stratified by demographic characteristics to mimic the most recent population census (BBS 2011): (1) households with children below 10 years old (40 percent), (2) households with elderly population (15 percent), and (3) mixed households (45 percent).
5. Devices used were Flow 2 by Plume Labs. Benchmarking the Flow 2 against approximately 14,000 static reference monitors (such as the FEM GRIMM and FEM T640), spread globally, suggests an average accuracy of the devices ranging between 90 percent to 95 percent (Jauvion et al. 2020).
6. For both indoor and outdoor conditions, as the devices produce real-time figures, exposure readings were collected and averaged over a five-minute period during each collection episode.
7. Although there is no threshold below which there is no impact on health, WHO recommends exposure to no higher than 15 micrograms per cubic meter ($\mu g/m^3$) of $PM_{2.5}$ and 45 $\mu g/m^3$ of PM_{10} over a 24-hour period. See the glossary for further details.

REFERENCES

BBS. 2011. Bangladesh Population Census 2011. Dhaka: Bangladesh Bureau of Statistics, Ministry of Planning, Government of Bangladesh.

GoB (Government of Bangladesh). 2018. *Ambient Air Quality in Bangladesh*. Dhaka: Ministry of Environment, Forest, and Climate Change. http://doe.portal.gov.bd/sites/default/files /files/doe.portal.gov.bd/page/cdbe516f_1756_426f_af6b_3ae9f35a78a4/2020-06-10-11-02 -5a7ea9f58497800ec9f0cea00ce7387f.pdf.

Jauvion, G., T. Cassard, B. Quennehen, and D. Lissmyr. 2020. DeepPlume: Very High-Resolution Real-Time Air Quality Mapping. Paris: Plume Labs. https://deepai.org/publication /deepplume-very-high-resolution-real-time-air-quality-mapping.

WHO (World Health Organization). 2021. *WHO Global Air Quality Guidelines: Particulate Matter (PM2.5 and PM10), Ozone, Nitrogen Dioxide, Sulfur Dioxide and Carbon Monoxide*. Geneva: WHO. https://apps.who.int/iris/handle/10665/345329.

3 Findings from the Household Survey

INTRODUCTION

The chapter provides an overview of the pollution levels recorded using the personal air quality measurement devices across the different study sites. It includes details of short-term illnesses as reported by the respondents using a 14-day recall period, noncommunicable diseases (NCDs) using a 12-month recall period, and mental health conditions using a 14-day recall period. Lastly, the chapter provides correlation estimates short-term illnesses such as productive cough, breathing difficulties and lower respiratory tract infections and individual, household, and locational characteristics.

EXPOSURE TO AIR POLLUTANTS

Figure 3.1 shows the respondent-level, weighted exposure to five pollutants—particulate matter 1 (PM_1), $PM_{2.5}$, PM_{10}, nitrogen dioxide (NO_2), and volatile organic compounds (VOCs)— across the four study sites.[1] The exposure to PM_1 ranged between 26.9 micrograms per cubic meter ($\mu g/m^3$) to 29.9 $\mu g/m^3$. The highest levels were reported in locations with major construction and heavy traffic while the lowest were in areas with persistent traffic. Locations with major construction and persistent traffic experienced the highest levels of $PM_{2.5}$ and PM_{10} (38 $\mu g/m^3$ and 60 $\mu g/m^3$, respectively). Consistent with information presented in the previous chapter, the lowest instance of both these pollutants (27 $\mu g/m^3$ and 31 $\mu g/m^3$, respectively) was recorded at the comparator location, Sylhet. Nitrogen dioxide (NO_2) and VOCs follow a similar pattern, where locations with major construction and persistent traffic report highest levels of both—20 parts per billion (ppb) and 17 ppb, respectively. The highest levels of NO_2 were reported by locations near brick kilns (17 ppb) while the comparator location reported the lowest levels of exposure to VOCs (117 ppb).

FIGURE 3.1

Weighted exposure to air pollutants, by study site

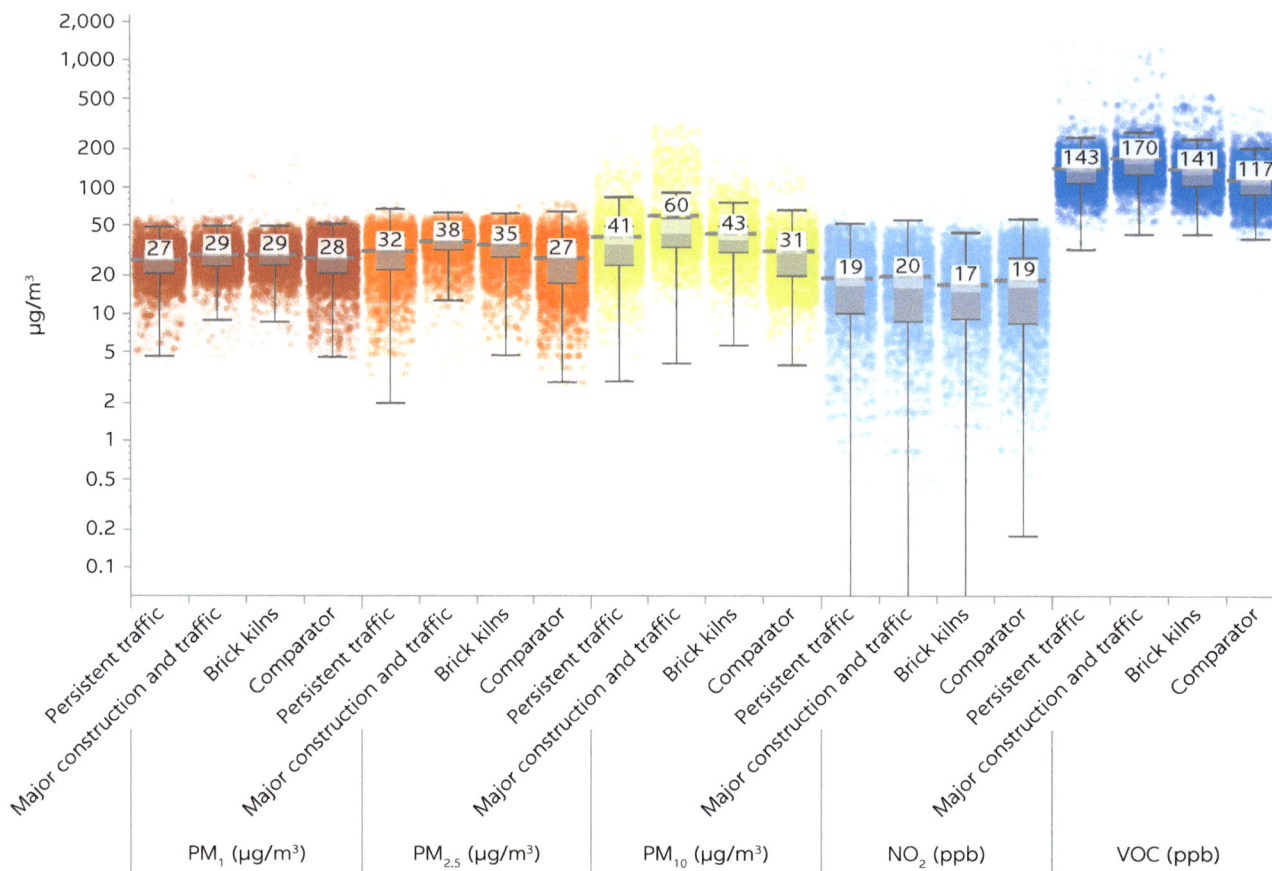

Source: Based on original calculations for this publication.
Note: The surveyed households were stratified across four sites reflecting the varying levels of pollution: (1) persistent traffic in the North and South Dhaka City Corporation areas, (2) major construction and persistent traffic in North and South Dhaka City Corporation areas, (3) brick kilns in the outskirts of Dhaka city, and (4) comparator site in rural Sylhet, one of the least polluted locations in the country. The gray bars show the average exposure to pollutants by study site. Each dot represents a respondent in the survey. The figures are weighted by the amount of time an individual spends in indoor and outdoor conditions. The personal air quality measurement devices used to collect data on exposure to air pollutants produce real-time readings (see the first section of chapter 2). The data for both outdoor and indoor readings were measured twice a day during specific times, a day before and on the day of the survey. The figure in each pane represents the average and the box plot shows the range between the 25th and 75th percentiles. The y axis is in a logarithmic form. Means tests across study sites are presented in appendix B table B.1. PM = particulate matter. PM numbers indicate the size of particles: PM_1 indicates particles of 1 micrometer, and so forth. NO_2 = nitrogen dioxide. ppb = parts per billion. $\mu g/m^3$ = micrograms per cubic meter. VOC = volatile organic compound.

As discussed earlier, this study limits all subsequent analyses to $PM_{2.5}$ and PM_{10}, the two major air pollutants that have the most impact on health. To foster a more intuitive understanding of exposure levels, the pollution levels are normalized as a percent increase (or decrease) from the World Health Organization's (WHO's) 2021 Air Quality Guidelines (AQG) (WHO 2021) over a 24-hour period ($15\mu g/m^3$ for $PM_{2.5}$ and $45 \ \mu g/m^3$ for PM_{10}; see the glossary). Average respondent-level exposure to $PM_{2.5}$ and PM_{10} is presented in figure 3.2. Exposures to $PM_{2.5}$ are highest in locations with major construction and persistent traffic—approximately 150 percent above WHO's 2021 AQG or equivalent to smoking 1.7 cigarettes per day (assuming no exposure to air pollution).[2] This is followed

FIGURE 3.2

Weighted exposure to air pollutants, by study site, compared to WHO Air Quality Guidelines

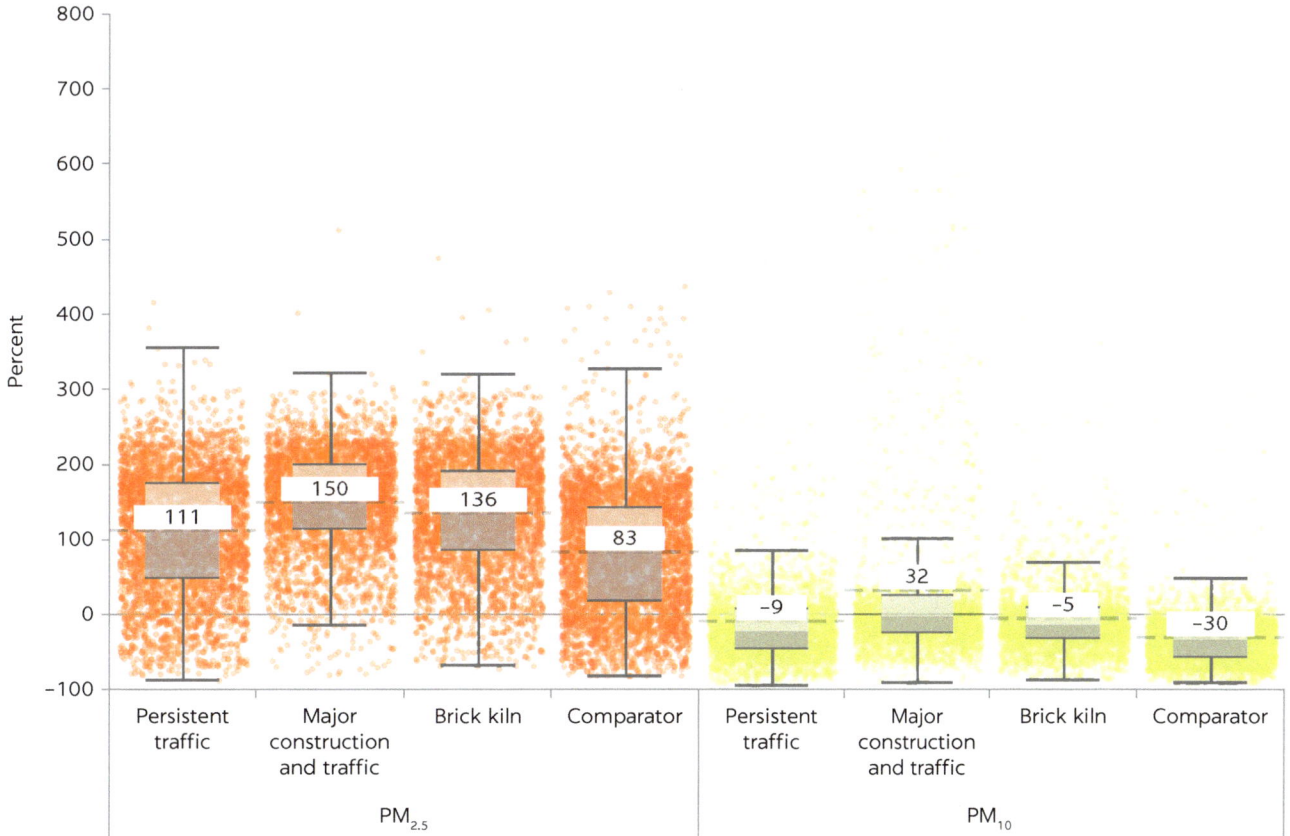

Source: Based on original calculations for this publication.
Note: The figure shows the weighted average exposure to $PM_{2.5}$ and PM_{10} by study site. Each dot represents a respondent in the survey. The figures are weighted by the amount of time an individual spends in indoor and outdoor conditions. The air pollution levels are presented as a percentage above (or below) the World Health Organization's (WHO's) 2021 Air Quality Guidelines (AQG). The figure in each pane represents the average and the box plot shows the range between the 25th and 75th percentiles. Means tests across study sites are presented in appendix B, table B.3. The surveyed households were stratified across four sites reflecting the varying levels of pollution: (1) persistent traffic in the North and South Dhaka City Corporation areas, (2) major construction and persistent traffic in North and South Dhaka City Corporation areas, (3) brick kilns in the outskirts of Dhaka city, and (4) comparator site in rural Sylhet, one of the least polluted locations in the country. PM = particulate matter. PM numbers indicate the size of particles: $PM_{2.5}$ indicates particles of 2.5 micrometers, and so forth.

by locations with brick kilns, where this is an average exposure of 136 percent above WHO's 2021 AQG, or equivalent to smoking 1.6 cigarettes per day (assuming no exposure to air pollution). While the levels are the lowest in the comparator location, the exposure to $PM_{2.5}$ remains 83 percent above WHO's 2021 AQG, or equivalent to smoking 1.2 cigarettes per day (assuming no exposure to air pollution). Concurrently, the greatest exposure to PM_{10}, approximately 32 percent above WHO's 2021 AQG, is experienced by respondents living in locations with major construction and persistent traffic. People living near brick kilns, however, experienced less exposure to PM_{10}, approximately 5 percent below WHO's 2021 AQG, while in the comparator areas, exposure to PM_{10} was the lowest (30 percent below WHO's 2021 AQG). Exposure across the primary sampling units (PSUs) are further illustrated in map 3.1.

MAP 3.1

Exposure to PM$_{2.5}$ and PM$_{10}$

a. Major construction and traffic

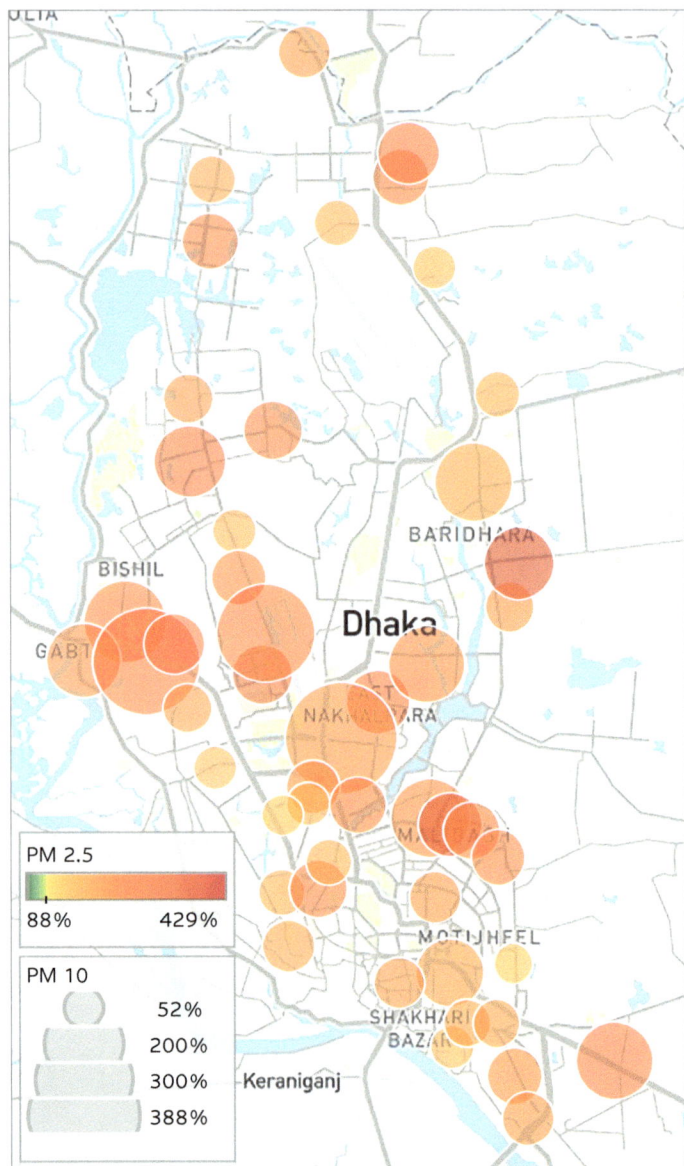

b. Kilns

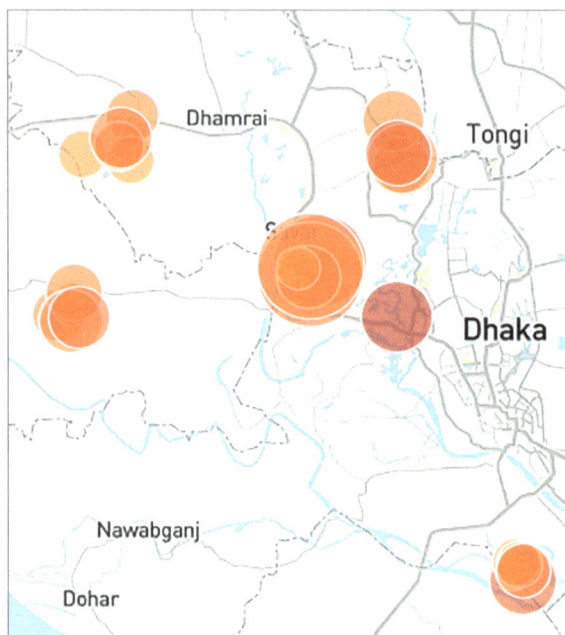

c. Comparator area

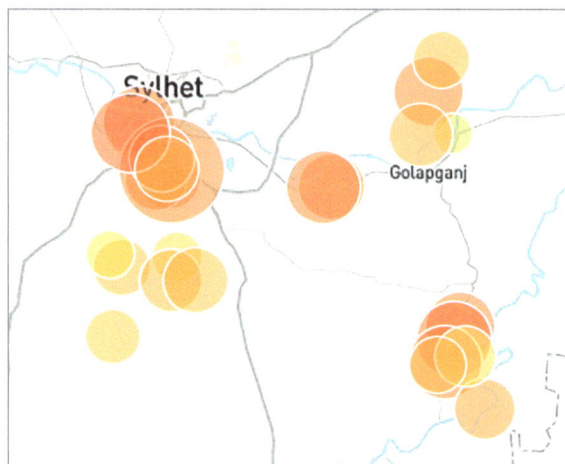

PM 2.5

88%   429%

PM 10

52%
200%
300%
388%

Source: Based on original calculations for this publication.
Note: PM = particulate matter. PM numbers indicate the size of particles: PM$_{2.5}$ indicates particles of 2.5 micrometers, and so forth. The figures show the average exposure to PM$_{2.5}$ and PM$_{10}$, aggregated at the primary sampling unit level. The air pollution levels are presented as a percentage above (or below) WHO's 2021 Air Quality Guidelines (AQG). The surveyed households were stratified across four sites reflecting the varying levels of pollution: (1) persistent traffic in the North and South Dhaka City Corporation (DCCs) areas, (2) major construction and persistent traffic in North and South Dhaka City Corporation areas, (3) brick kilns in the outskirts of Dhaka city, and (4) a comparator site in rural Sylhet, one of the least polluted locations in the country. Panel a shows locations with major construction and traffic in Dhaka North and South City Corporations. Panel b shows locations in the outskirts of DCCs with brick kilns. Panel c shows the comparator location in rural Sylhet.

The differentials between indoor and outdoor exposure conditions are also revealing (see appendix B figure B.3). Conforming to expectations, the exposure levels to PM$_{2.5}$ and PM$_{10}$ are notably lower indoors than outdoors in locations with persistent traffic. In locations with major construction and persistent traffic, the difference between the average indoor and outdoor exposure to PM$_{2.5}$ is comparable—254 percent and 246 percent, respectively. Whereas for PM$_{10}$,

FIGURE 3.3

Pollution and socioeconomic status

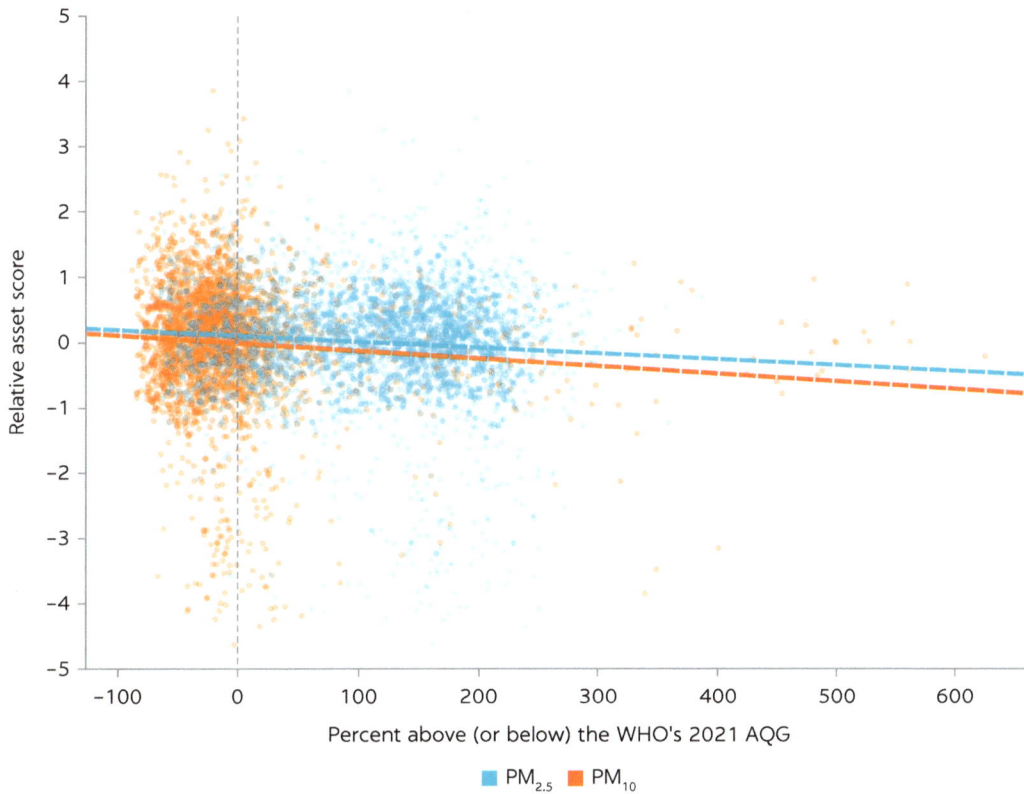

Percent above (or below) the WHO's 2021 AQG

■ PM$_{2.5}$ ■ PM$_{10}$

Source: Based on original calculations for this publication.
Note: The figure shows the relationship between exposure to pollution particles (PM$_{2.5}$ and PM$_{10}$) and relative continuous socioeconomic status using a fitted linear curve (bivariate linear model) at the individual level. The air pollution levels are presented as a percentage above (or below) the World Health Organization's 2021 Air Quality Guidelines over a 24-hour period. The slopes of PM$_{2.5}$ and PM$_{10}$ both are significant below the 1 percent level, indicating a statistically significant negative relationship. AQG = Air Quality Guidelines; PM = particulate matter; WHO = World Health Organization. PM numbers indicate the size of particles: PM$_{2.5}$ indicates particles of 2.5 micrometers, and so forth.

the exposure levels indoors are in fact higher than outdoors—138 percent versus 120 percent. While the trends of exposure for those living near brick kilns are comparable to those in locations with persistent traffic, the indoor and outdoor conditions in the comparator location do not vary.

Figure 3.3 shows the relationship between a continuous relative socioeconomic status score and pollutants PM$_{2.5}$ and PM$_{10}$ using a bivariate linear method. The slope coefficients of PM$_{2.5}$ and PM$_{10}$ are 0.089 and −0.117, both with p-values below the 1 percent level. This suggests that a higher relative socioeconomic status (by one point of the asset score) is associated with reduced exposure to pollutants PM$_{2.5}$ and PM$_{10}$ by 8.9 and 11.7 percentage points (or 45 and 91 percent), respectively.

SHORT-TERM ILLNESSES

This section analyzes several self-reported illnesses or conditions experienced by the respondents, which are associated with short-term exposure to air pollution. These are cough (includes gradations such as the presence of sputum and/or blood), breathing difficulties with or without accompaniment by wheezing sounds, fever (duration and with or without chills), eye problems (redness, burning sensations, wateriness, or itching), and skin conditions (rashes, hives, itching, acne, or dermatitis).

Figure 3.4 shows the proportion of respondents reporting these conditions across the study sites. Overall 13.8 percent reported experiencing a cough in the 14-days preceding the survey, with the highest proportions (15.5 percent) in locations near brick kilns and 14.2 percent living near major construction sites and traffic. Of the 4 percent reporting breathing difficulties across the sample, the highest proportion (5.3 percent) are from those living near major construction sites with persistent traffic. Approximately 19.2 percent of the sample experienced a fever over the recall period, of which the highest was among those living near brick kilns. Approximately 9 percent of the respondents experienced eye problems and 8 percent reported skin conditions. In all instances, the highest proportion were reported among those living near brick kilns.

Figure 3.5 shows the proportion of respondents across age groups suffering a health condition. Among those who reported experiencing a cough in the 14-day

FIGURE 3.4

Short-term illnesses (14-day recall), by study site

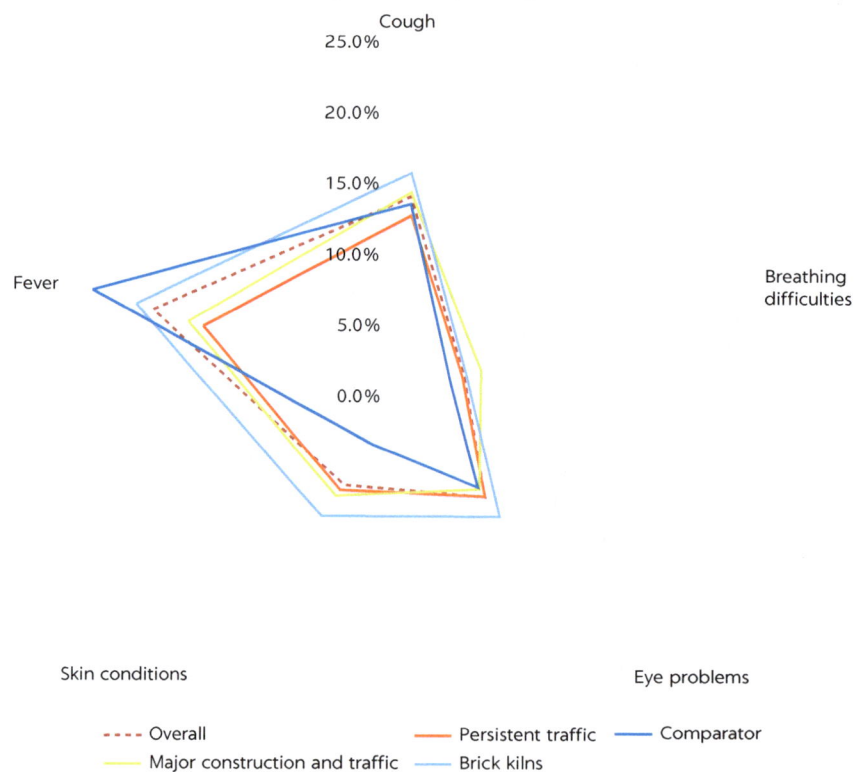

Source: Based on original calculations for this publication.
Note: The figure shows the distribution of air-pollution-related illnesses experienced by respondents using a 14-day recall period. Dotted line represents the mean for the whole sample. Eye problems include redness, burning sensations, wateriness, or itching; skin conditions include rashes, hives, itching, acne, or dermatitis. Means tests across study locations are presented in appendix B table B.5. The surveyed households were stratified across four sites reflecting the varying levels of pollution: (1) persistent traffic in the North and South Dhaka City Corporation areas, (2) major construction and persistent traffic in North and South Dhaka City Corporation areas, (3) brick kilns in the outskirts of Dhaka city, and (4) comparator site in rural Sylhet, one of the least polluted locations in the country.

FIGURE 3.5

Short-term illnesses (14-day recall), by age groups

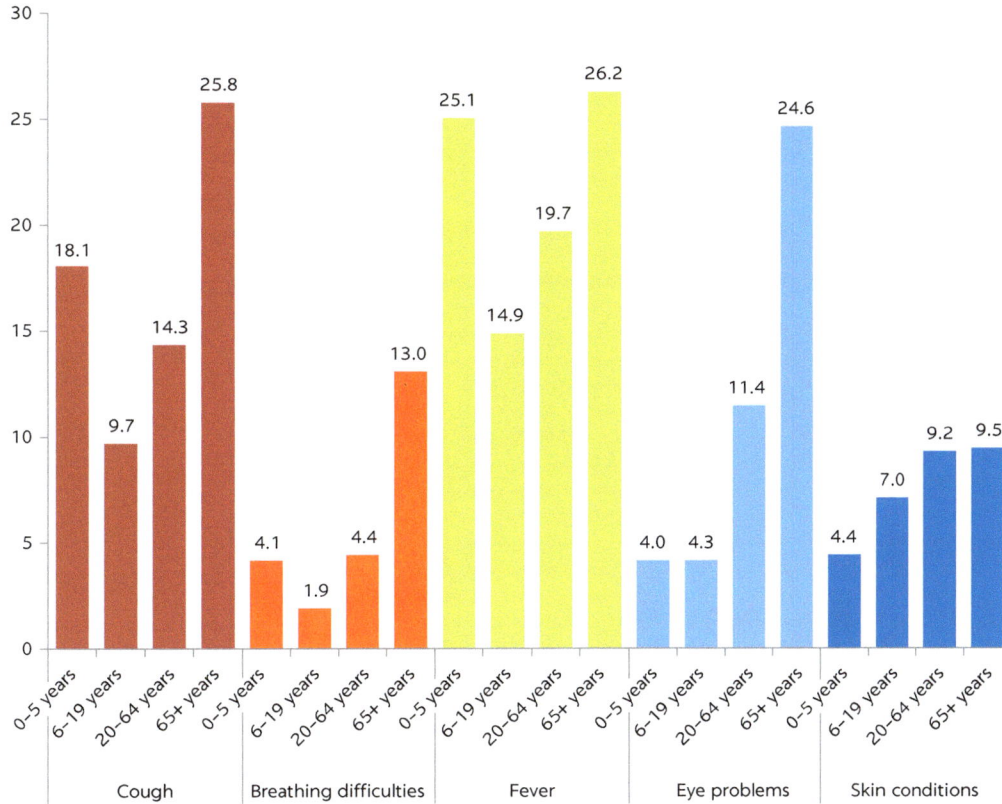

Source: Based on original calculations for this publication.
Note: Figure shows the distribution of air pollution related illnesses experienced by respondents using a 14-day recall. Eye problems include redness, burning sensations, wateriness, or itching. Skin conditions include rashes, hives, itching, acne, or dermatitis. Means tests across gender are presented in appendix B table B.5. Means tests across age groups are presented in appendix B table B.5.

period preceding the survey, the highest numbers were reported by the elderly (65 years and older) followed by children (0 to 5 years)—25.8 percent and 18.1 percent, respectively. The elderly also experienced the highest burden (13.0 percent) when it comes to experiencing breathing difficulties, fever (26.2 percent), eye problems (24.6 percent), and skin conditions (9.5 percent). For skin conditions such as rashes, hives, itching, acne, or dermatitis, the elderly and adults (20 to 64 years) were most susceptible (9.5 percent) while the lowest incidences were reported by children 0 to 5 years (4.4 percent).

Figure 3.6 outlines the trends in these illnesses by gender. The difference between the genders when it comes to experiencing cough of breathing difficulties was negligible. A higher proportion of women reported having a fever during the 14-days preceding the survey than men (20.7 percent versus 17.5 percent). Similarly, 10.6 percent of women reported having an eye problem compared to 7.4 percent men.

Figure 3.7 shows the trends in experienced illnesses by socioeconomic status. Approximately 17.9 percent of the richest reported a cough followed by 13.6 percent of the poorest. The difference in proportion of individuals who experienced breathing difficulties among the richest and the poorest is negligible (approximately 4.9 percent 4.8 percent, respectively). The richest also reported the highest rates of fever (21.1 percent) followed by the poorest (20.2 percent).

FIGURE 3.6
Short-term illnesses (14-day recall), by gender identity

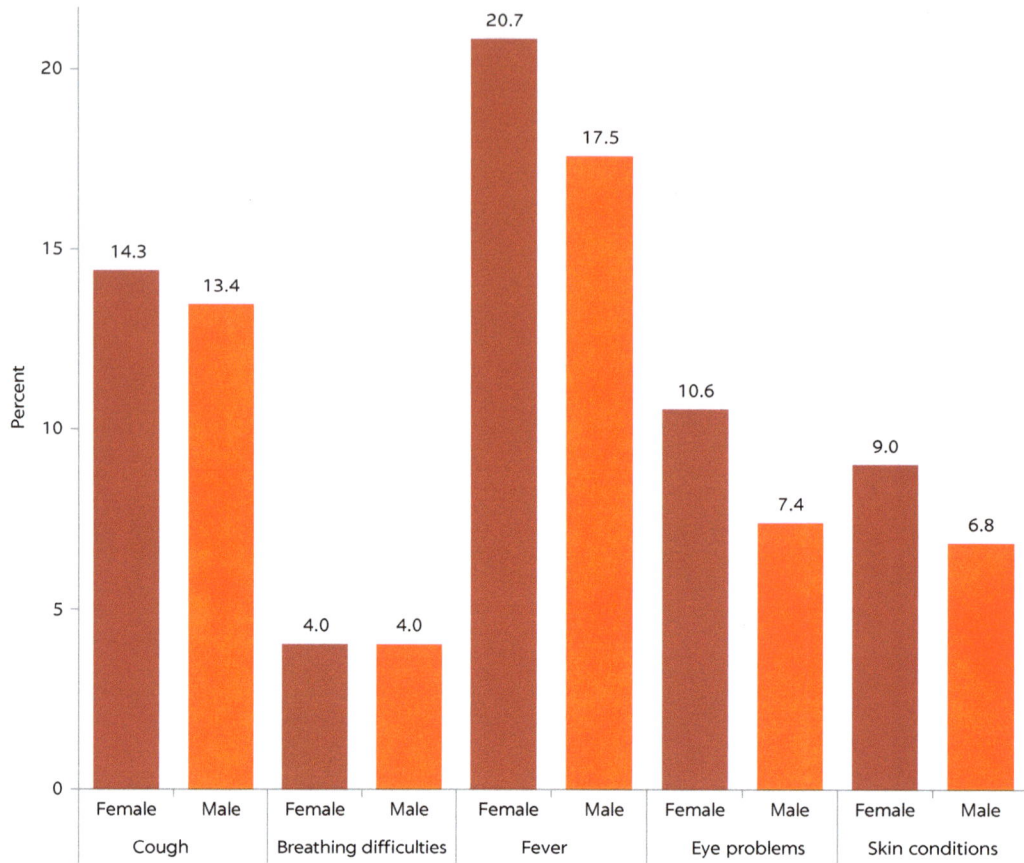

Source: Based on original calculations for this publication.
Note: The figure shows the distribution of air-pollution-related illnesses experienced by respondents using a 14-day recall. Eye problems include redness, burning sensations, wateriness, or itching. Skin conditions include rashes, hives, itching, acne, or dermatitis. Means tests across gender are presented in appendix B table B.5.

Around 10.3 percent of the richest reported an eye problem, followed by 9.5 percent among the poorest. Skin conditions were experienced by the richest (11.6 percent) much more than those in the lower wealth quintiles. Overall, for all types of illnesses, the proportion is the highest among the richest, followed by the poorest.

The survey also assessed prevalence of COVID-19 among the respondents. Approximately 0.19 percent of the all respondents experienced COVID-19, with the highest proportions of respondents living in areas with brick kilns (0.27 percent), major construction and persistent traffic (0.24 percent), persistent traffic (0.2 percent), and comparator (0.06 percent). As expected, the rates were highest among the elderly (65 years and older) at 0.47 percent, followed by adults (20 to 64 years) and adolescents (6 to 19 years).

FIGURE 3.7

Short-term illnesses (14-day recall), by socioeconomic status

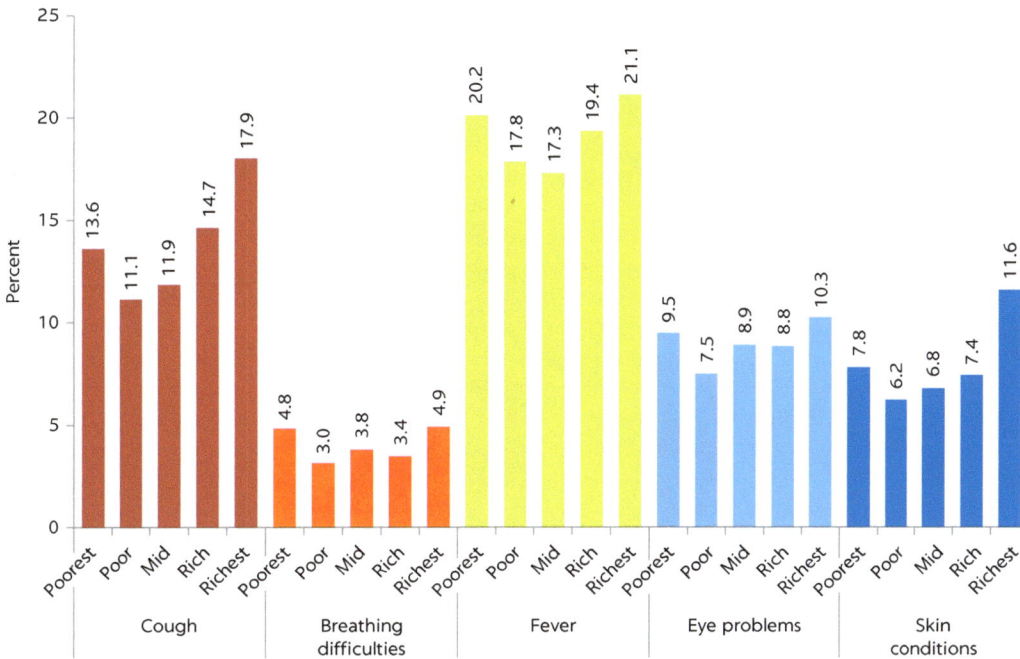

Source: [Based on original calculations for this publication.
Note: The figure shows the distribution of air-pollution-related illnesses experienced by respondents using a 14-day recall. Eye problems include redness, burning sensations, wateriness, or itching. Skin conditions include rashes, hives, itching, acne, or dermatitis. Means tests across socioeconomic status are presented in appendix B table B.5.

LOWER RESPIRATORY TRACT INFECTIONS

Using a series of cascading questions that leverages information collected on the symptoms and illnesses experienced by the respondent over a 14-day period preceding the survey, the study assigns scores in conjunction with a cut-off point above which the individual is considered to have a lower respiratory tract infection. The symptoms and illnesses used to construct this scoring mechanism are detailed in appendix B table B.11. The condition was not substantiated by a radiological test and, therefore, is *indicative* of the presence of the infection.

Figure 3.8 shows the proportion of individuals with a lower respiratory tract infection for the full sample and across the study sites. Overall, 13.9 percent of the respondents reported a lower respiratory tract infection with the highest proportion of respondents (16.1 percent) living near brick kilns. This is followed by respondents living in locations with major construction and persistent traffic (14.2 percent), the comparator site (13.0 percent), and those with persistent traffic (12.4 percent). Disaggregation by age groups suggests that the elderly (65 years and older) experience the highest burden of lower respiratory tract infections, at 28.8 percent (see figure 3.9). They are followed by children (0 to 5 years) and adults (20 to 64 years), with prevalence of 15.2 percent each. Women, in general, report a higher proportion of lower respiratory tract infections (14.9 percent) than men (12.7 percent).

FIGURE 3.8

Proportion of individuals with lower respiratory tract infections, by location

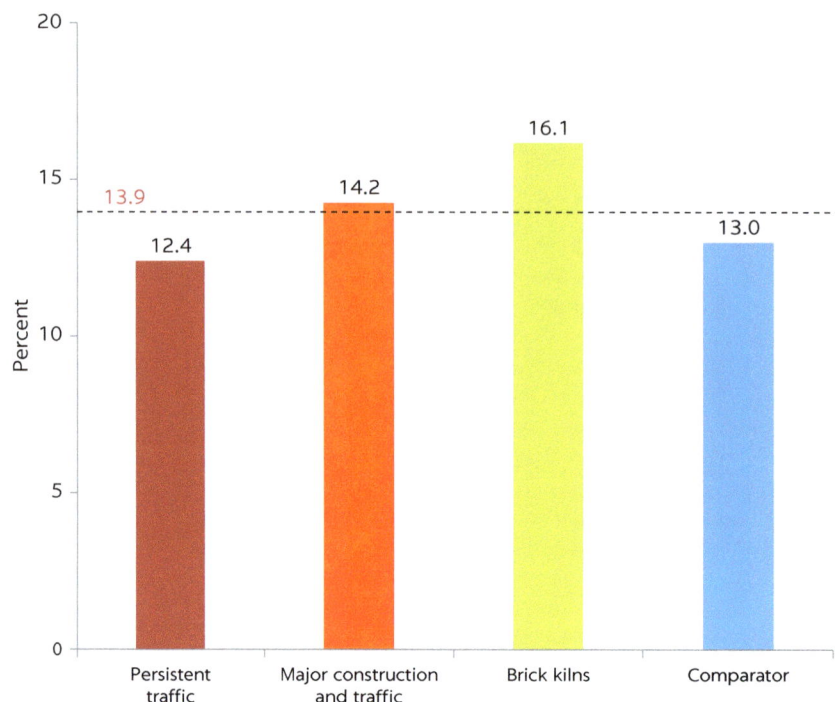

Source: Based on original calculations for this publication.
Note: The figure is calculated as the proportion of individuals who scored at least 6 in the Respiratory Infection Score, indicating a likely presence of a lower respiratory tract infection (see appendix B table B.2 for the scoring system). The condition was not substantiated by a radiological test and, therefore, is *indicative* of the presence of the infection. Dotted line represents overall mean for the full sample. Means tests across study locations are presented in appendix B table B.6. The surveyed households were stratified across four sites reflecting the varying levels of pollution: (1) persistent traffic in North and South Dhaka City Corporation areas, (2) major construction and persistent traffic in North and South Dhaka City Corporation areas, (3) brick kilns in the outskirts of Dhaka city, and (4) comparator site in rural Sylhet, one of the least polluted locations in the country.

Figure 3.10 further breaks down the prevalence of the proportion of individuals with lower respiratory tract infections, stratified by age groups and location. Among children between 0 and 5 years, the highest prevalence of lower respiratory tract infections are reported by those living in locations with major construction and traffic (17.2 percent), followed closely by those living near brick kilns (17.1 percent). In line with expectations, children living in comparator sites report the lowest rates (12.9 percent). The highest proportions reporting a lower respiratory tract infection were among adolescents (6 to 19 years) and adults (20 to 64 years) who live near brick kilns (10.1 percent and 18.4 percent, respectively). Comparably to children, the highest reported instances of the condition among the elderly were those living in locations with major construction and traffic (33.3 percent), followed by those living in the comparator sites (30.8 percent). The proportion of the elderly living in locations with persistent traffic or near brick kilns reported the lowest incidences of the condition—25.7 percent and 25.5 percent, respectively.

FIGURE 3.9
Proportion of individuals with lower respiratory tract infections, by demographic status

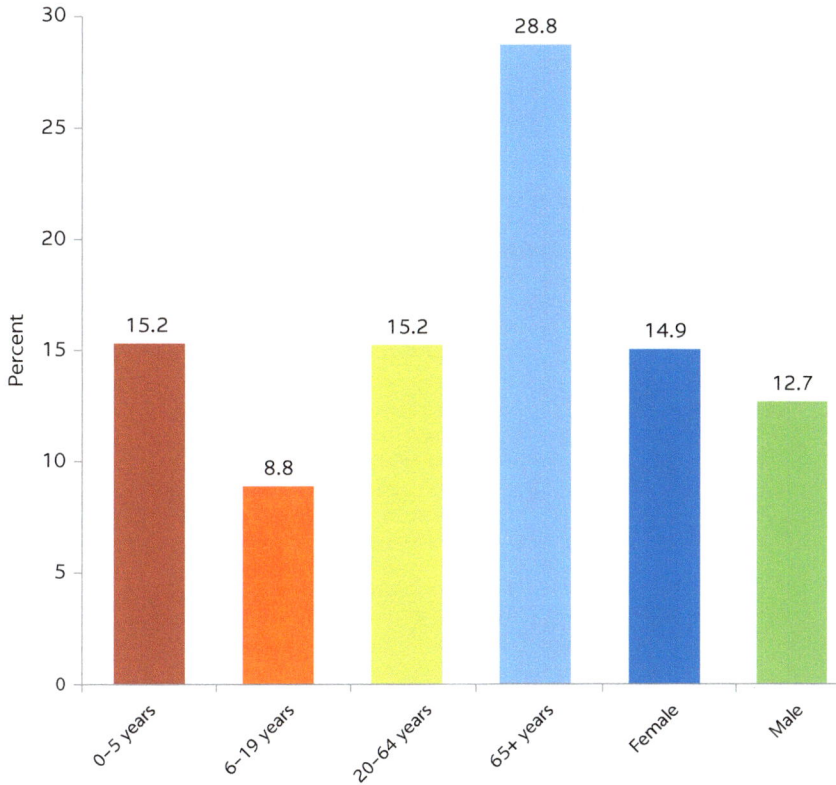

Source: Based on original calculations for this publication.
Note: The figure is calculated as the proportion of individuals who scored at least 6 in the Respiratory Infection Score (see appendix B, table B.2), suggesting a lower respiratory tract infection. The condition was not substantiated by a radiological test and, therefore, is *indicative* of the presence of the infection. Means tests across demographic characteristics are presented in appendix B table B.6. The surveyed households were stratified across four sites reflecting the varying levels of pollution: (1) persistent traffic in the North and South Dhaka City Corporation areas, (2) major construction and persistent traffic in North and South Dhaka City Corporation areas, (3) brick kilns in the outskirts of Dhaka city, and (4) comparator site in rural Sylhet, one of the least polluted locations in the country. Means tests across study locations are presented in appendix B table B.6.

The relationship between exposure to $PM_{2.5}$ and PM_{10} and the (continuous) Respiratory Infection Score using a bivariate linear method is presented in figure 3.11. Slopes of $PM_{2.5}$ (blue line) and PM_{10} (orange line) have coefficients of 0.107 and 0.073, the former with a p-value below the 5 percent level. This suggests that a one percent increase in the exposure to $PM_{2.5}$ above WHO's 2021 AQG, increases the probability of the Respiratory Infection Score (that is, experiencing a lower respiratory tract infection by one point) by 10.7 percentage points.

NONCOMMUNICABLE DISEASES

This section discusses the prevalence of NCDs experienced by respondents in the 12 months preceding the survey. The conditions were mentioned by the respondents as diagnosed by medical professionals.

FIGURE 3.10

Proportion of individuals with lower respiratory tract infections, by location and age

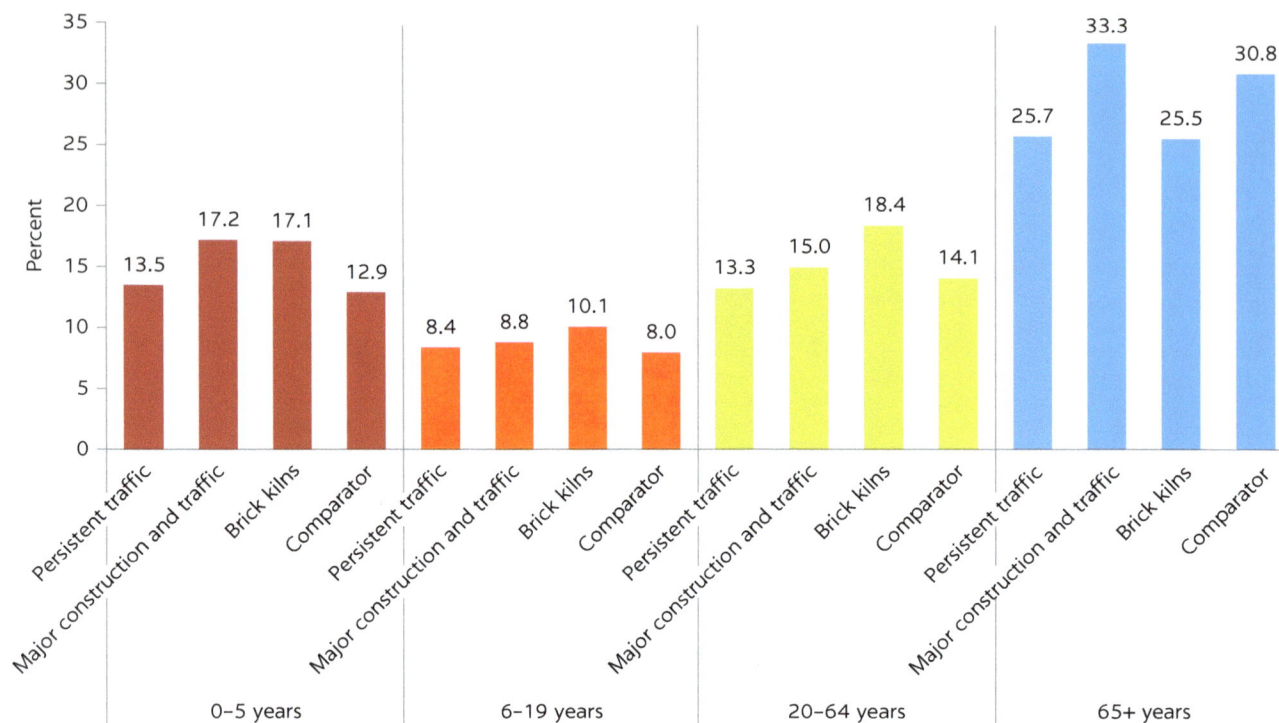

Source: Based on original calculations for this publication.

Note: The figure is calculated as the proportion of individuals who scored at least 6 in the Respiratory Infection Score, a likely presence of a lower respiratory tract infection (see appendix B, table B.2 for the scoring scheme). The condition was not substantiated by a radiological test and, therefore, is *indicative* of the presence of the infection. Means tests across study locations are presented in appendix B table B.6. The surveyed households were stratified across four sites reflecting the varying levels of pollution: (1) persistent traffic in the North and South Dhaka City Corporation areas, (2) major construction and persistent traffic in North and South Dhaka City Corporation areas, (3) brick kilns in the outskirts of Dhaka city, and (4) comparator site in rural Sylhet, one of the least polluted locations in the country.

Figure 3.12 shows the prevalence of the NCDs across the four study sites. Approximately 16.6 percent of respondents reported suffering from allergies, with the highest proportion (19.4 percent) in areas with brick kilns and the lowest (14.6 percent) in the comparator site. Of those who suffered from an allergy (table 3.1), the top three variations include food allergies (68.5 percent), dust allergies (39.1 percent), and allergies to mold (4.2 percent).

On average, diabetes was reported by 4.0 percent of the respondents, and observations did not vary significantly across the four study sites. Similarly, approximately 2.3 percent of the respondents reported experiencing a heart condition, and the proportion did not vary significantly across the study sites. With regard to hypertension, the highest proportion was reported by those living in the comparator site (9.6 percent) and the lowest (6.3 percent) in locations with major construction and persistent traffic.

Chronic or persistent respiratory problems were reported by approximately 1.8 percent of the respondents. Those living in areas with persistent traffic reported the highest proportions (2.4 percent) while the lowest were in comparator site (1.3 percent). Approximately 1.0 percent of the respondents experienced a stroke during the 12 months preceding the survey. Of this sample, the highest reported rates (1.2 percent) are from comparator site (1.4 percent), while the lowest are from locations near brick kilns (0.7 percent).

FIGURE 3.11
FIGURE 3.11
Relationship between pollutants and lower respiratory tract infection

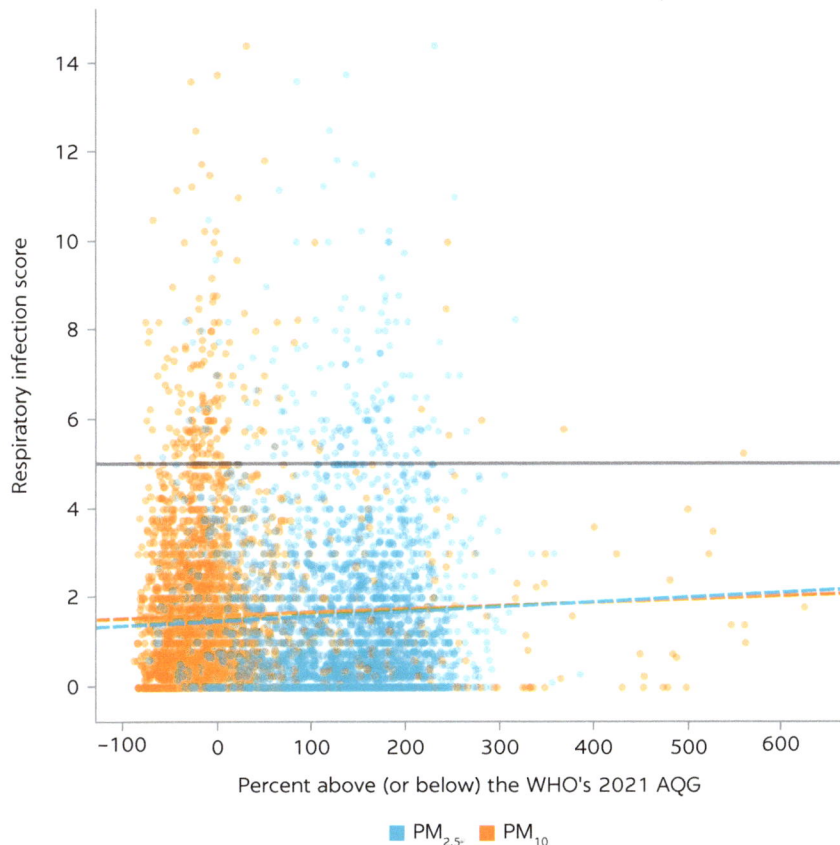

Source: Based on original calculations for this publication.
Note: The figure shows the relationship between air pollutants (x-axis) and Respiratory Infection Score (y-axis) using a fitted linear curve (bivariate linear model) at the individual level. Exposure to $PM_{2.5}$ and PM_{10} are presented as a percentage above (or below) the World Health Organization's 2021 Air Quality Guidelines, over a 24-hour period. Respondents with a Respiratory Infection Score above 5 (dotted line) are likely to have a lower respiratory tract infection in the 14 days preceding the survey, but this has not substantiated by radiology test and, therefore, is indicative and not clinically proven. The slope of $PM_{2.5}$ is significant below the 5 percent level, indicating a statistically significant positive relationship. AQG = Air Quality Guidelines; PM = particulate matter; WHO = World Health Organization. PM numbers indicate the size of particles: $PM_{2.5}$ indicates particles of 2.5 micrometers, and so forth.

Figure 3.13 shows the distributions of the NCDs, stratified by age groups. Allergies span well across each of the age groups. The highest reported rates were from adults (20 to 64 years) and the elderly (65 or more years). Approximately 6.3 percent of the children reported suffering from an allergy, the lowest among the age groups. As expected, diabetes is the highest among the elderly) and nearly three times higher than adults—17.1 percent versus 6.0 percent. Similarly, hypertension and stroke rates are the highest among the elderly, at least three times higher than among adults.

Figure 3.14 shows the distribution of NCDs by gender. The prevalence of these conditions is higher among women than men. Approximately 17.9 percent of the women in the sample reported allergies compared to 15.0 percent among the men; diabetes is higher among women than men (4.6 percent versus 3.3 percent); and chronic respiratory conditions is also higher among women

FIGURE 3.12

Prevalence of noncommunicable diseases (NCDs), by study site

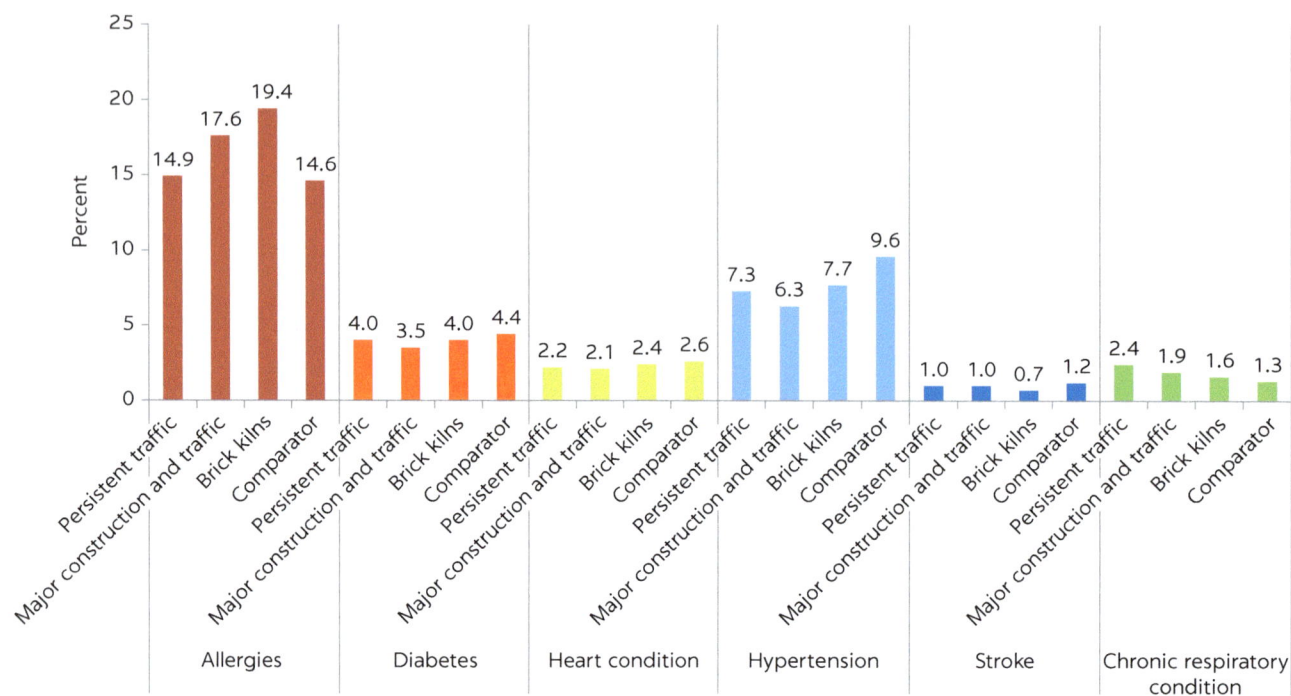

Source: Based on original calculations for this publication.
Note: The figure shows the means of NCDs, as diagnosed by a medical professional, using a 12-month recall period. Means tests across study locations are presented in appendix B table B.7. The surveyed households were stratified across four sites reflecting the varying levels of pollution: (1) persistent traffic in the North and South Dhaka City Corporation areas, (2) major construction and persistent traffic in North and South Dhaka City Corporation areas, (3) brick kilns in the outskirts of Dhaka city, and (4) comparator site in rural Sylhet, one of the least polluted locations in the country.

TABLE 3.1 **Highest reported allergies**

Food allergy	68.5%
Dust allergy	39.1%
Mold allergy	4.2%

Source: Based on original calculations for this publication.
Note: Responses restricted to individuals who reported suffering from allergies.

(1.9 percent) than men (1.7 percent). While the proportion of individuals with heart conditions does not vary significantly by gender, the rate of hypertension is markedly higher among women than men (9.2 percent versus 6.2 percent). Perhaps an anomaly in contrast to other conditions, stroke is nearly three times higher among men than women—1.4 percent versus 0.6 percent.

Figure 3.15 shows the distribution of the NCDs across the socioeconomic status of the respondents. Those in the richest wealth quintile report the highest rates of all morbidities, while generally the lowest rates are reported by those in the poorest quintile. With regard to allergies, the proportion among the richest is nearly twice as among the poorest (22.2 percent versus 13.3 percent). Similarly, 8 percent of the richest report having diabetes compared to only 2.3 percent among the poorest. A similar trend is noted for heart diseases, hypertension, and stroke. On the other hand, the proportion of respondents reporting chronic respiratory conditions is comparably more evenly distributed than other diseases. Approximately 2.5 percent of the richest report experiencing such conditions, while the same is true for 2.0 percent of those in the poorest socioeconomic quintile.

FIGURE 3.13

Prevalence of noncommunicable diseases (NCDs), by age

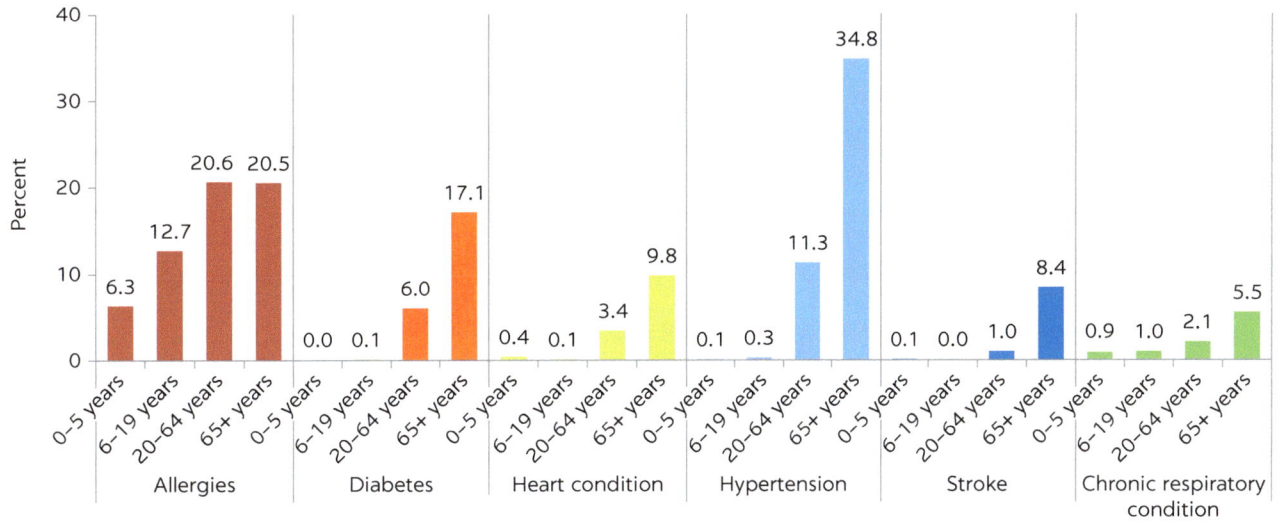

Source: Based on original calculations for this publication.
Note: The figure shows the means of NCDs, as diagnosed by a trained medical professional, using a 12-month recall period. Means tests across age groups are presented in appendix B table B.7.

FIGURE 3.14

Prevalence of noncommunicable diseases (NCDs), by gender identity

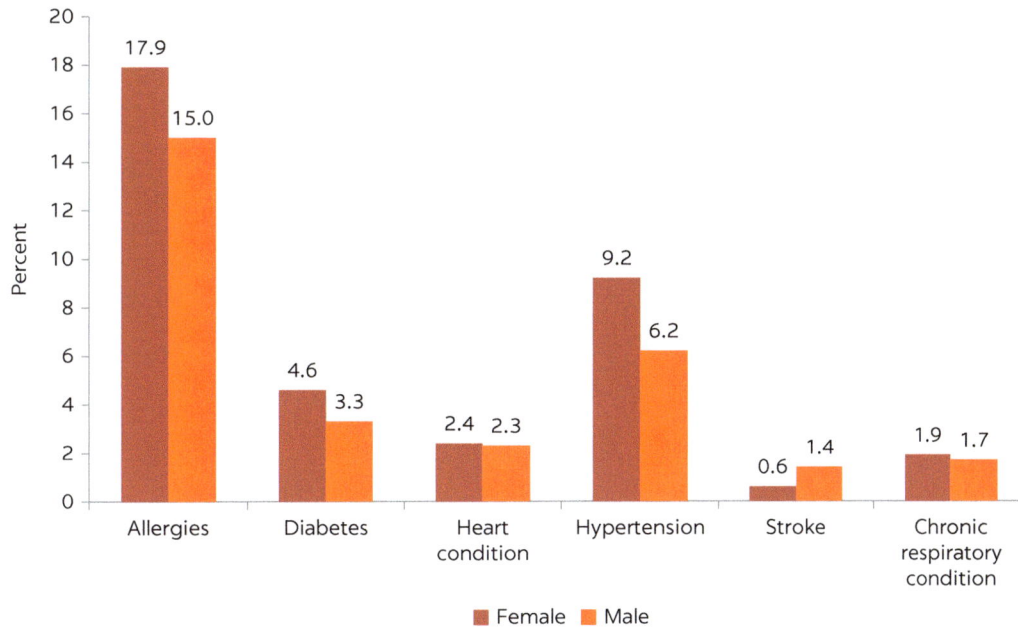

Source: Based on original calculations for this publication.
Note: The figure shows the means of NCDs, as diagnosed by a trained medical professional, using a 12-month recall period. Means tests across gender identity are presented in appendix B, table B.7.

FIGURE 3.15

Prevalence of noncommunicable diseases (NCDs), by socioeconomic status

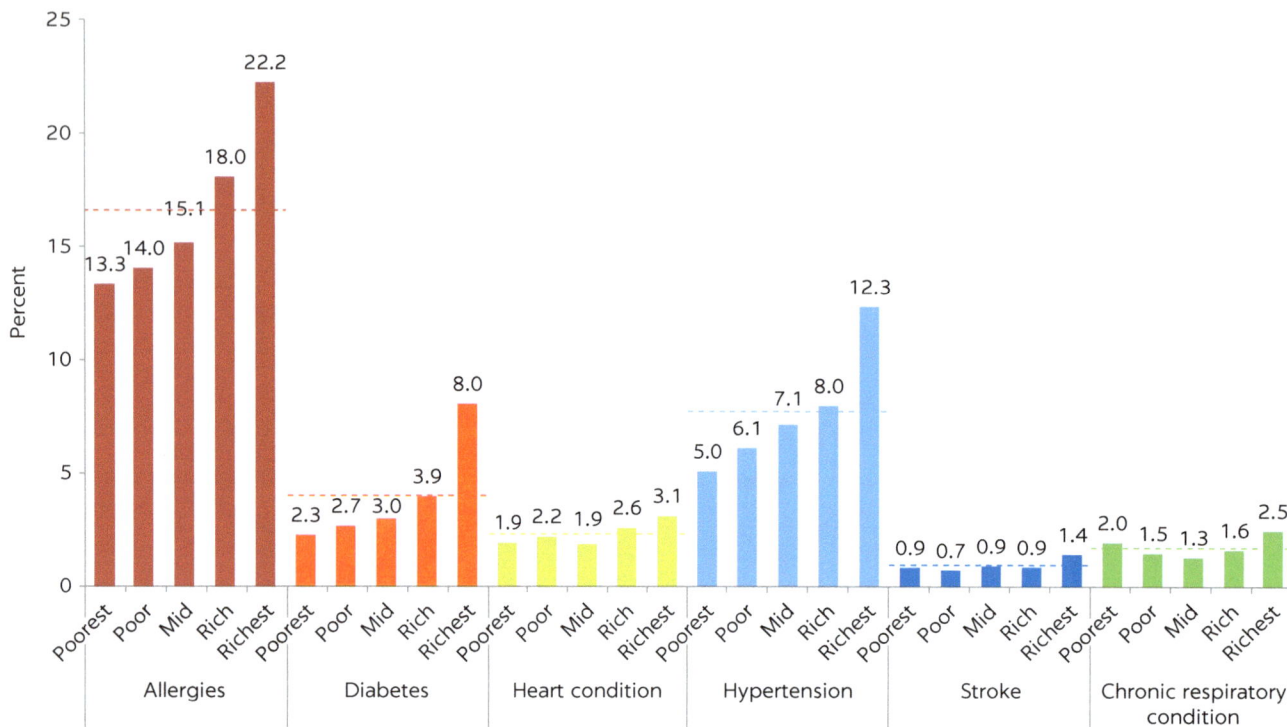

Source: Based on original calculations for this publication.
Note: The figure shows the means of NCDs, as diagnosed by a trained medical professional, using a 12-month recall period. Dotted line shows the average for each NCD. Means tests across socioeconomic status are presented in appendix B, table B.7.

The relationship between exposure to pollutants $PM_{2.5}$ and PM_{10} and prevalence of chronic respiratory conditions is explored at the PSU level using a bivariate linear method (see figure 3.16). Slopes of $PM_{2.5}$ (blue line) and PM_{10} (orange line) have coefficients of 0.003 and 0.005, the latter with a p-value below the 10 percent level. This suggests that a 1 percent increase in the exposure to PM_{10} above WHO's 2021 AQG (see the glossary) raises the probability of having chronic respiratory conditions increasing in the PSUs by 0.5 percent.

CORRELATES OF PRODUCTIVE COUGH, BREATHING DIFFICULTIES, AND RESPIRATORY INFECTIONS

This section explores factors correlated with the probability of a respondent experiencing a productive cough, breathing difficulties, or having a lower respiratory tract infection. The heterogeneity of these conditions by demographic characteristics and presence of comorbidities across the study sites is also analyzed.

Productive cough

Overall, exposure to $PM_{2.5}$ is significantly associated with productive cough. Column 3 in figure 3.2 shows the factors associated with a respondent experiencing a productive cough with thick sputum. A 1 percent increase in the exposure

FIGURE 3.16
FIGURE 3.16

Relationship between pollutants and chronic respiratory conditions

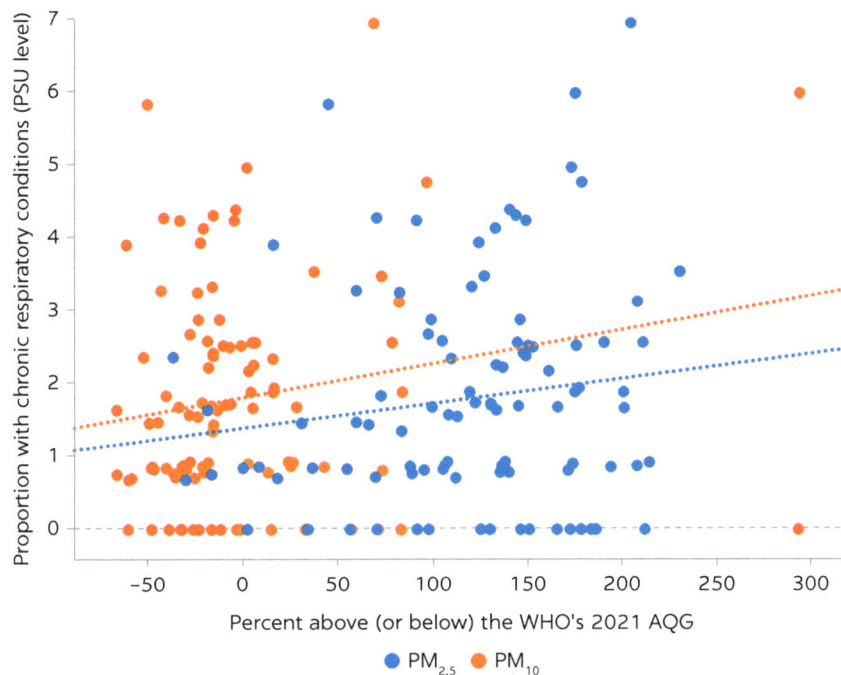

Source: Based on original calculations for this publication.
Note: The figure shows the relationship between air pollutants (x-axis) and chronic respiratory conditions at the PSU-level (y-axis) using a fitted linear curve (bivariate linear model). Exposure to $PM_{2.5}$ and PM_{10} is presented as a percentage above (or below) the World Health Organization's 2021 air Quality Guidelines over a 24-hour period. The slope of PM_{10} is significant below the 10 percent level, indicating a statistically significant positive relationship. AQG = Air Quality Guidelines; PM = particulate matter; WHO = World Health Organization. PM numbers indicate the size of particles: $PM_{2.5}$ indicates particles of 2.5 micrometers, and so forth; PSU = primary sampling unit.

to $PM_{2.5}$ over WHO's 2021 AQG increases the probability of a respondent experiencing productive cough by 12.5 percent. Appendix B table B.8 shows detailed outputs, while results from the heterogeneity analysis are provided in appendix B table B.9.

In terms of demographic characteristics, children (0 to 5 years) and the elderly (65 or more years) are more likely to experience productive cough than adults ages 20 to 65 years (the reference group). The odds of reporting a productive cough are 59.7 percent higher for children and 169.9 percent higher for the elderly than adults. Heterogeneity of effects across study sites show some notable results. For instance, children living in areas with major construction and persistent traffic have 88.3 percent higher odds of reporting a productive cough than children living in the comparator site (see appendix B table B.9). In parallel, children in locations with brick kilns are 47.4 percent less likely to report a productive cough than children living in areas with major construction and persistent traffic (see appendix B table B.9). Notably, children living in locations with major construction and persistent traffic are more likely to have productive coughs than those living near brick kilns or comparator locations. The number of hours spent in outdoor conditions and increasing socioeconomic status are positively associated with the probability of reporting a productive cough.

Exposure to outdoors by an additional hour increases the probability of reporting a productive cough by 2.3 percent. While the vulnerability does not vary by gender identity, a larger household size is associated with lower chances of experiencing a productive cough (4.9 percent). A higher socioeconomic status is negatively associated with the condition. Except for those in the highest quintile, people in higher quintiles are progressively less likely to report a productive cough than the poorest.

Medically confirmed comorbidities in individuals during the 12 months preceding the survey increase the odds of reporting a productive cough. Those with allergies are 188.1 percent more likely to report a productive cough than those without. Similarly, individuals who report having diabetes (66.3 percent), heart conditions (63.1 percent), or stroke (76.4 percent) are more likely to experience a productive cough than those who do not. Individuals who have had a stroke during the recall period are at a significantly higher risk of reporting the condition (580 percent) than those who have not. Comparison of individuals with allergies or having had a stroke or living near bricks kilns have 39.7 percent and 91 percent lower odds, respectively, of reporting a productive cough than those living near major construction sites with persistent traffic— see appendix B table B.9. Overall, individuals with comorbidities such as allergies or having had a stroke have lower odds of reporting a productive cough when they live close to brick kilns than locations with major construction and persistent traffic.

Breathing difficulties

Location plays a strong predictive role for respondents suffering breathing difficulties. Individuals living in locations with persistent traffic and major construction and persistent traffic alone have significantly higher odds of experiencing breathing difficulties than those living in comparator locations— by 41.1 percent and 65.1 percent, respectively. Exposure to $PM_{2.5}$ plays a similar role—a 1 percent increase in exposure over WHO's 2021 AQG is associated with a 12.8 percent increase in the probability of experiencing breathing difficulties. Factors associated with an individual experiencing breathing problems in the 14 days preceding the survey are presented in table 3.2. (Appendix B table B.8 shows detailed outputs, while results from the heterogeneity analysis are provided in appendix B table B.10.)

Children (0 to 5 years) are 70.3 percent and the elderly (65 or more years) 197 percent more likely to report breathing difficulties than adults (20 to 64 years). Moreover, children living in locations with major construction and persistent traffic are more susceptible to breathing difficulties than others. The odds of these children experiencing the condition living in locations with major construction and traffic are 237.4 percent higher when compared to those living in comparator location and 63.7 percent higher in contrast to those living in locations with persistent traffic (see appendix B table B.10). The living near brick kilns have a lower probability of experiencing breathing difficulties than those living in the comparator sites (see appendix B table B.10).

Socioeconomic status is negatively associated with the probability of experiencing breathing difficulties—compared to the poorest, the poor and the rich have 34.4 percent and 32.6 percent lower probabilities, respectively. As with productive coughs, comorbidities play a large role in respondents experiencing breathing difficulties over a 12-month recall period. Individuals with allergies are 250.4 percent more likely to experience this condition than those without. Moreover, individuals with allergies living in areas with major construction and persistent traffic are 127.9 percent more likely than those in the comparator areas and 42.1 percent less likely than those near brick kilns to experience breathing difficulties (see appendix B table B.10). Conditions such as diabetes (77.4 percent) and heart diseases (237.6 percent) are also associated with a higher risk of experiencing breathing difficulties.

Overall, individuals living in locations with persistent traffic and with major construction and persistent traffic are more susceptible to experiencing breathing difficulties than those in comparator locations. Exposure to $PM_{2.5}$ is significantly and positively associated with breathing difficulties. The elderly (65 or more years) and children (0 to 5 years) are more likely to report breathing difficulties than adults (20 to 64 years). Analysis of heterogeneity across locations suggests that children living near major construction sites and persistent traffic are more vulnerable than those living elsewhere. Socioeconomic status is negatively associated with the likelihood of the condition. Comorbidities such as allergies, diabetes, and heart conditions are strongly associated with breathing difficulties. Notably, individuals with allergies living in locations with major construction and traffic are at higher risk of having breathing difficulties than those living near brick kilns or in the comparator locations.

Lower respiratory tract infection

Individuals living in traffic-prone areas are 25.2 percent less likely to report a lower respiratory tract infection than those in the comparator site. In parallel, a 1 percent increase in exposure to $PM_{2.5}$ over WHO's 2021 AQG increases the odds of a lower respiratory tract infection by 8.1 percent. Factors associated with respondents experiencing a lower respiratory tract infection is presented in table 3.2. (Appendix B table B.8 shows detailed outputs, and results from the heterogeneity analysis are provided in appendix B table B.11.) The Respiratory Infection Score was used to determine whether an individual is likely experiencing a lower respiratory tract infection (as described in the first section of chapter 2 and appendix B table B.2) and not substantiated by radiological tests.

Age plays a determining role in experiencing a lower respiratory tract infection. Children (0 to 5 years) are 97.9 percent more likely to suffer from a lower respiratory tract infection than adults (20 to 64 years). Assessment of the heterogeneity across the study site shows that children living in locations with major construction and traffic have 137 percent greater odds of experiencing a lower respiratory tract infection than children living in the comparator site. In parallel, children living in locations with persistent traffic or near brick kilns are less likely to report a lower respiratory tract infection than children living in the presence of major construction and persistent traffic, by 37.9 percent and

TABLE 3.2 Correlates of having a productive cough, breathing problems, or a respiratory infection

Category	Variables	Productive cough	Breathing difficulties	Lower respiratory tract infection
Study sites (Comparator)	Persistent traffic	0.806	1.411**	0.748**
	Major construction and traffic	0.996	1.651***	0.929
	Brick kilns	1.027	1.177	0.943
Air pollutants (% of safe exposure)	$PM_{2.5}$	1.125**	1.128*	1.081*
	PM_{10}	1.005	1.066	1.033
Age (20–64 years)	0–5 years	1.597*	1.703*	1.979***
	6–19 years	0.738	0.659*	0.836
	65+ years	2.699***	2.970***	2.304***
Gender identity (Female)	Male	0.883	1.107	0.891
Time use	Hours spent outdoors	1.023**	1.015	1.015*
Activity (Outdoor low-skilled work)	Homemaker	0.854	0.831	0.697**
	Indoor low-skilled work	0.870	0.653	0.726*
	Indoor skilled work	0.854	0.710	0.641***
	Student	0.654	0.620	0.483***
	Other	0.786	0.687	0.645***
	None (children <5 years)	0.879	0.661	0.533***
Wealth quintiles (Poorest)	Poor	0.749**	0.656***	0.746***
	Mid	0.736**	0.791	0.745***
	Rich	1.055	0.674**	0.827***
	Richest	1.150	0.912	0.942
Household characteristics	Household size	0.951*	0.977	0.946**
	Improved stove used	1.005	0.858	0.988
Comorbidities	Allergies	2.881**	3.504***	2.714***
	Diabetes	1.663**	1.774***	1.627***
	Heart disease	1.631**	3.376***	1.736***
	Hypertension	0.991	1.232	1.109
	Stroke	1.764**	1.130	1.682**
		0.3 0.5 1.0 2.0 4.0	0.3 0.5 1.0 2.0 4.0	0.3 0.5 1.0 2.0 4.0
		Adjusted odds ratios	Adjusted odds ratios	Adjusted odds ratios

Source: Based on original calculations for this publication.

Note: The table shows adjusted odds ratios (AOR) from a logistic model. The binary dependent variables are whether a respondent has reported experiencing a productive cough with a thick sputum (column 3), experienced breathing problems (column 4) and is likely to have a lower respiratory tract infection (column 5) as calculated using relevant symptoms report in appendix B table B.8, using a 14-day recall period (not substantiated by radiology tests and hence not clinically proven). Base categories are reported in parentheses in the "Category" column. The surveyed households were stratified across four sites reflecting the varying sources levels of pollution: (1) persistent traffic in the North and South Dhaka City Corporation areas; (2) major construction and persistent traffic in North and South Dhaka City Corporation areas; (3) brick kilns in the outskirts of Dhaka city; and (4) comparator site in rural Sylhet, one of the least polluted locations in the country. The models account for primary sampling unit–level heterogeneity (output not reported) and report robust standard errors. The x-axis is in logarithmic form. Results are also interpretable as percentage changes ([AOR – 1] * 100 = Percentage Change). Detailed outputs from the model are presented in appendix B table B.8.

***, **, and * represent significance below the 1 percent, 5 percent, and 10 percent levels.

47.9 percent, respectively. (See appendix B table B.11 for further details.) The elderly (65 or more years) are 130.4 percent more likely to suffer from a lower respiratory tract infection than adults.

The type of primary activity plays a large role in determining whether an individual experiences a lower respiratory tract infection. Compared to those engaged in outdoor low-skilled work, all others appear to have greater protection against the condition. Higher socioeconomic status is negatively associated with the probability of having a lower respiratory tract infection; for instance, those in the rich quintile are 17.3 percent less likely to experience a lower respiratory tract infection than the poorest. Moreover, an additional hour outdoors is associated with a 1.5 percent increase in the odds of having a lower respiratory tract infection.

Medically confirmed comorbidities are significantly associated with the chances of having a lower respiratory tract infection. Individuals with allergies are 171.4 percent more likely to have experienced a lower respiratory tract infection than those without. Moreover, those with allergies living in locations with major construction and persistent traffic have a 42.8 percent higher chance of having a lower respiratory tract infection than individuals with allergies in the comparator area. The same is true for respondents with allergies living close to brick kilns—these individuals report 29.9 percent lower odds of having a lower respiratory tract infection than those living in locations with major construction and persistent traffic.

Respondents with comorbidities such as diabetes, heart conditions, and experience of a stroke have greater odds of experiencing a lower respiratory tract infection by 62.7 percent, 73.6 percent, and 68.2 percent, respectively. The likelihood among individuals with these comorbidities of having a lower respiratory tract infection is higher among respondents living near major construction sites with persistent traffic. (See appendix B table B.11.)

Overall, exposure to $PM_{2.5}$ is associated with experiencing a lower respiratory tract infection. Age plays a large determining role in the vulnerability to such infections. Among the age groups, children (0 to 5 years) and the elderly (65 or more years) are more vulnerable than adults (20 to 64 years), with the elderly likely to have this condition more than children. It is worthwhile to note that children living near sites with major construction and persistent traffic are far more vulnerable to lower respiratory tract infections than children living in any other location. People with comorbidities such as allergies, diabetes, heart conditions, or stroke have considerably higher odds of having a lower respiratory tract infection than those without. At the same time, individuals with allergies, diabetes, or heart conditions living near major construction sites with persistent traffic are more susceptible to the infection than those living elsewhere.

MENTAL HEALTH AND POLLUTION

This section discusses the prevalence of depression among respondents using a two-week recall. Depression levels were measured using the WHO-5 screening questionnaire and expressed as levels exceeding the threshold of 50.

Figure 3.17 shows the prevalence of depression across the study sites. Depression is most reported in locations with persistent traffic and areas of major construction and traffic (13.7 percent), while the lowest rates are reported among those living near brick kilns (11.2 percent).

Figure 3.18 shows the prevalence of depression across demographic characteristics. It is important to note that the age categorizations used to analyze depression are more granular than for the rest of the report, mostly driven by the fact that the WHO-5 is validated for those above 15 years of age and that the underpinning drivers of depressive symptoms vary by age groups. In line with expectations, depression increases with age, with those 65 years or older being particularly susceptible. Females are more depressed than men, 13.7 percent compared to 11.8 percent. The trends of increased depression with increasing age and a higher prevalence among females are in line with experiences in other countries, as documented in existing literature.

FIGURE 3.17

Prevalence of depression across study sites

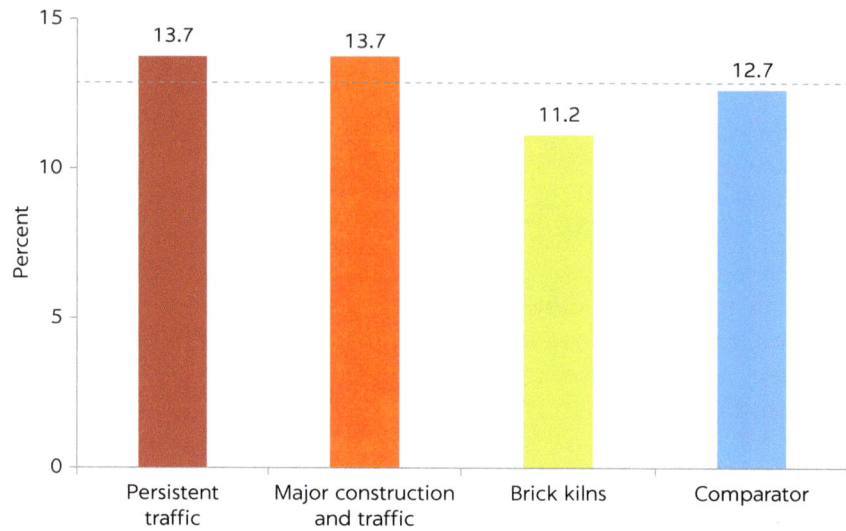

Source: Based on original calculations for this publication.
Note: The figure shows the prevalence of depression, determined using the WHO-5 depression screening tool. Individuals whose responses are below a cutoff score of 50 are considered depressed. The dotted line represents the mean for the full sample. Means tests across study locations are presented in appendix B table B.12. The surveyed households were stratified across four sites reflecting the varying sources and levels of pollution: (1) persistent traffic in the North and South Dhaka City Corporation areas, (2) major construction and persistent traffic in North and South Dhaka City Corporation areas, (3) brick kilns in the outskirts of Dhaka city, and (4) comparator site in rural Sylhet, one of the least polluted locations in the country.

FIGURE 3.18

Prevalence of depression across demographic characteristics

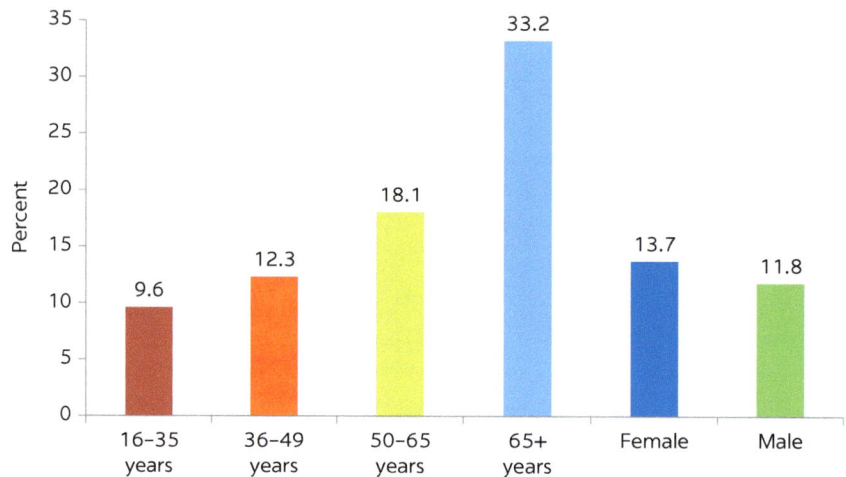

Source: Based on original calculations for this publication.
Note: The figure shows prevalence of depression, determined by using the WHO-5 depression screening tool (using a cutoff of ≤ 50), across demographic characteristics. Means tests across demographic characteristics are presented in appendix B table B.12.

Correlates of depression

Table 3.3 shows the correlates of depression using a multivariate logistic model (see appendix B table B.13 for further details). A 1 percent increase in exposure to $PM_{2.5}$ above WHO's 2021 AQG is associated with a 20 percent higher

TABLE 3.3 Correlates of depression

Category	Experiment	Adjusted odds ratio
Study sites (comparator)	Persistent traffic	1.050
	Major construction and trafic	0.955
	Brick kilns	0.762**
Air pollutants (% of WHO 2021 Air Quality Guidelines)	PM$_{2.5}$	1.202**
	PM$_{10}$	1.017
Age (15–35 years)	36–49 years	1.069
	50–65 years	1.395***
	65+	2.871***
Gender identity (Male)	Female	1.357***
Time use	Hours spent outdoors	1.032***
Education (none)	Primary	0.601***
	Secondary	0.673***
	High school	0.615***
	High school and above	0.637**
	Religious education	0.391*
Household characteristics	Improved fuel	1.027
	Household size	0.897
Wealth quintiles (Poorest)	Poor	0.835*
	Mid	0.736***
	Rich	0.637***
	Richest	0.583***
Short-term illnesses	Breathing difficulties	1.561***
	Cough	1.089
	Fever	1.217**
	Respiratory infection	1.263
Comorbidities	Allergies	1.082
	Diabetes	1.134
	Heart disease	1.377**
	Hypertension	1.251**
	Stroke	2.772***

Adjusted odds ratios (x-axis scale: 0.2, 0.5, 1.0, 2.0, 5.0)

Source: Based on original calculations for this publication.
Note: The figure shows adjusted odds ratios (AORs) from a logistic model. The binary dependent variable is whether a respondent is depressed as per the World Health Organization-5 scale. Robust standard errors are calculated using the Huber-White approach (1967). Results are interpretable as percentage changes ([AOR − 1] * 100 = percentage change). The surveyed households were stratified across four sites reflecting the varying sources levels of pollution: (1) persistent traffic in the North and South Dhaka City Corporation areas, (2) major construction and persistent traffic in North and South Dhaka City Corporation areas, (3) brick kilns in the outskirts of Dhaka city, and (4) comparator site in rural Sylhet, one of the least polluted locations in the country. ***, **, and * represent significance below the 1 percent, 5 percent, and 10 percent levels.

probability of the individual reporting being depressed, while no association is found with exposure to PM_{10}. Residing in areas with persistent traffic and areas with major construction and traffic were not associated with increased likelihood of depression compared to the comparator sites. Interestingly and somewhat counterintuitively, those residing in areas near brick kilns have a 24 percent lower chance of depression than the comparator areas. While each hour spent outdoors increased the likelihood of depression by 3 percent, there was no statistically significant relationship detected between the type of cooking fuel used and depression. Association between other confounding factors and depression (including age, gender identity, educational attainment, socioeconomic status, underlying health conditions, and so forth) has also been explored and the findings are in line with existing literature (Mahmud, Raza, and Hossain 2021).

The findings show exposure to $PM_{2.5}$ in Bangladesh to be contributing to depression, as are the number of hours a person spends outdoors—taken together, this indicates a possible vulnerability of aggravated depression levels with worsening air quality, as time spent outdoors is usually associated with well-being and reduced adverse mental health outcomes. A recently conducted systematic review of studies from across the world utilizing meta-analysis methods did not find a statistically significant relationship of exposure to $PM_{2.5}$ and PM_{10} (short term and long term) with depression but cited methodological limitations and the need for additional research to further examine this relationship (Fan et al. 2020). A recent systematic review exploring the connection between $PM_{2.5}$ exposure and depression found a significant association, indicating depression increasing with higher levels of exposure to $PM_{2.5}$ (Braithwaite et al. 2019). Collectively, the lack of consensus evident from these reviews indicates the need for further research into the effects of exposure of air pollutants on mental health outcomes. Accordingly, the current report is a valuable contribution as an entry point in the scientific knowledge surrounding this relationship in Bangladesh, where previously there were no known estimations.

NOTES

1. The pollutants are weighted by the numbers of hours the respondents spent exposed to indoor and outdoor conditions. The breakdown of outdoor and indoor levels of pollutants are presented in appendix B figures B.1 and B.2. PM numbers indicate the size of particles: PM_1 indicates particles of 1 micrometer in diameter, and so forth.
2. One cigarette per day is the rough equivalent of a $PM_{2.5}$ level of 22 µg/m³ exposure to air pollution (Echenique 2018).

REFERENCES

Braithwaite, I., S. Zhang, J. B. Kirkbride, D. P. J. Osborn, and J. F. Hayes. 2019. "Air Pollution (Particulate Matter) Exposure and Associations with Depression, Anxiety, Bipolar, Psychosis and Suicide Risk: A Systematic Review and Meta-Analysis." *Environmental Health Perspectives* 127 (12). https://doi.org/10.1289/EHP4595.

Echenique, M. 2018. "How Much Are You 'Smoking' by Breathing Urban Air?" *Bloomberg*, April 25, 2018. https://www.bloomberg.com/news/articles/2018-04-25/the-app-that-translates-air-pollution-into-cigarettes.

Fan, S. J., J. Heinrich, M. S. Bloom, T. Y. Zhao, T. X. Shi, W. R. Feng, Y. Sun, et al. 2020. "Ambient Air Pollution and Depression: A Systematic Review with Meta-Analysis up to 2019." *Science of the Total Environment* 20 (701): 134721. doi:10.1016/j.scitotenv.2019.134721.

Huber, Peter J. 1967. "The Behavior of Maximum Likelihood Estimates under Nonstandard Conditions." Proceedings of the Fifth Berkeley Symposium on Mathematical Statistics and Probability. Vol. 5: 21–233.

Mahmud, I., W. A. Raza, and Md. R. Hossain. 2021. *Climate Afflictions*. International Development in Focus. Washington, DC: World Bank. https://openknowledge.worldbank .org/handle/10986/36333.

WHO (World Health Organization). 2021. *WHO Global Air Quality Guidelines: Particulate Matter (PM2.5 and PM10), Ozone, Nitrogen Dioxide, Sulfur Dioxide and Carbon Monoxide*. Geneva: WHO. https://apps.who.int/iris/handle/10665/345329.

4 Conclusions and the Way Forward

INTRODUCTION

Bangladesh is extremely vulnerable to the effects of air pollution, with an estimated 78,145 to 88,229 deaths in 2019 alone, caused by exposure to fine particulate matter with a diameter of 2.5 micrometers ($PM_{2.5}$) (World Bank, forthcoming). Bangladesh was ranked as the most polluted country in the world and its capital Dhaka as the second most polluted city each year between 2018 and 2021 (IQAir 2021).[1] Moreover, between 2009 and 2019, four of the five top causes of total deaths in Bangladesh were directly associated with air pollution.[2] The economic cost of these impacts on health is huge, estimated between 3.9 and 4.4 percent of Bangladesh's gross domestic product in 2019 (World Bank, forthcoming).

Although there is global evidence linking air pollution and its effect on health, evidence from Bangladesh is limited. Moreover, the evidence that is available is constrained by narrow geographical coverage, conducted with small, nonrepresentative samples, or a lack of localized granular air pollution data that can effectively establish the link between air pollution and health. One of the important prerequisites to addressing these gaps is to first understand the contextual extent of the problem: that is, understanding the levels of air pollution in various parts of Bangladesh, and next, establishing how exposure to air pollutants interacts with and affects human health.

This report, the first of its kind from Bangladesh, provides evidence on the short-term effects of ambient air pollution on human health. The analysis, guided by existing literature, is based on individual- and household-level primary data on health conditions, localized air pollution data collected during the survey, and historical data from across the country on air pollution levels. The main highlights of the report are the following:

- Dhaka is the most polluted division, while Sylhet is the least polluted in Bangladesh. The western side of the country appears to be more polluted than the eastern parts.
- Sites with major construction and persistent traffic are the largest sources of ambient air pollution rather than brick kilns, as commonly believed.

- The elderly, children, and individuals with underlying health conditions are more vulnerable than others to the health risks associated with ambient air pollution.
- There is a direct association between exposure to ambient air pollution and impact on human health.

To mitigate the impacts of air pollution, the Department of Environment's Air Pollution Reduction Strategy for Bangladesh 2012 stipulates specific measures to reduce emission levels, promote the use of improved technologies to improve air quality, and establish institutional reforms for coordination and governance. In 2019, Bangladesh drafted the Clean Air Bill, which will help prepare the National Air Quality Management Plan and identify critical air quality areas (HEI 2020). More recently, in September 2021, the government of Bangladesh released the Mujib Climate Prosperity Plan Decade 2030, which shifts the discourse on climate change from "vulnerability to resilience to prosperity" for the country. Priority areas and points emphasized by the plan are (1) accelerating adaptation to the effects of climate change; (2) transitioning labor and future-proofing industry with technology transfer; (3) increasing public revenue to spend on the most vulnerable members of the population; (4) establishing comprehensive climate and disaster risk financing and management; (5) leveraging twenty-first century technologies for human well-being; and (6) maximizing renewable energy, energy efficiency, and power and transportation sector resilience.

With air pollution levels anticipated to worsen over time in Bangladesh, driven by climate change as well as factors such urbanization and industrialization, there is an urgent need for the health sector to be better prepared to deal with the impending crisis. It is expected that the report will assist practitioners and subject matter experts in policy dialogue under the overall framework of the government's Mujib Climate Prosperity Plan Decade 2030.

While measures to reduce the impact of climate change would contribute to tackling air pollution, the following summarized recommendations are linked to the findings presented in this report and are not aimed at managing air pollution in general.

ADAPTIVE MEASURES FOR CONSIDERATION BY THE HEALTH SECTOR

The following may be undertaken under the leadership of the Ministry of Health and Family Welfare, in collaboration with relevant stakeholders, including the local government.

Recommendation 1: Improve health service delivery to deal with the health effects of air pollution, with a focus on vulnerable groups such as the elderly and children. Curative care, particularly delivered through public health platforms, needs to be further strengthened to treat the health problems brought on by air pollution. Doing this would help ease the additional and incremental burden of health expenditure on the population. The following measures can be implemented as a part of the efforts to strengthen the health care delivery system:

- Increase awareness of and sensitivity of health care professionals to the health risks associated with exposure to ambient air pollution.

- Enhance the capacity of medical practitioners through targeted training to detect and treat air-pollution-driven morbidity.
- Institute a mainstream response to deal with mental health issues through the provision of community-based solutions for prevention and treatment. These can include, for instance, the creation of peer support groups at local community levels.
- Training nonspecialists to detect and treat common mental disorders.

Recommendation 2: Strengthen public health response mechanism to promote preventive measures. Community-level screening for specific conditions such as persistent coughs and breathing difficulties among people living in areas with relatively high air pollution levels ("hot spots") will assist the government in detecting and addressing emerging health issues. The following actions can be considered to achieve this goal:

- Establish community-level mobile teams to screen for health risks associated with air pollution. These teams should work in shifts and be available during the evening to cover the population not available during the day.
- Prioritize the screening of the elderly and children, who are more susceptible to the effects of air pollution.
- Create awareness among the general population about the adverse effects on health due to air pollution through outreach activities using community health workers and volunteers.
- Mobilize communities, local leaders, and social influencers to promote preventive actions such as regular use of face masks, which can reduce inhalation of harmful pollutants to an extent.
- Identify areas with relatively high air pollution as hot spots where these actions need to be prioritized.

ADAPTIVE MEASURES IMPLEMENTED THROUGH A MULTISECTORAL APPROACH

The Ministry of Environment, Forest, and Climate Change may be well positioned to lead this multisectoral approach in consultation with stakeholders.

Recommendation 3: Record more granular and localized data with high fidelity to monitor air pollution levels closely. Together with the weather data (on temperature, humidity, and precipitation) collected by the Bangladesh Meteorological Department, the agencies will be able to provide a fuller picture of the extent of air pollution in Bangladesh. Actions to be implemented are the following:

- Increase the number of continuous air-monitoring stations throughout the country to collect more localized and granular information on the various air pollutants.
- Strengthen capacity to capture additional data points using updated technology. Geostationary operational environmental satellites-R series and the joint polar satellite system monitor the particle pollution in the atmosphere. These track smoke particles from wildfires, airborne dust during dust- and sandstorms, urban and industrial pollution, and ash from erupting volcanoes (SciJinks n.d.).
- Use existing sources of information, coupled with localized ground-level information, to continually monitor the impact of air pollution on human health. Such evidence should be used for decision-making purposes.

- Establish effective public outreach systems to provide early warning during days expected to have high air pollution levels.

Recommendation 4: Conduct further research to substantiate the effects of air pollution on health as well to establish the nexus between climate change and air pollution. This report provides a litany of information, but additional work in this space will help triangulate the findings and assist in better understanding the health impacts of air pollution. Accordingly, policy makers should be supported in undertaking evidence-based actions. Actions that can be implemented are the following:

- Collect repeated time-series data on air pollution as well as on specific health issues that are influenced by air pollution from a larger sample over a longer time horizon. The availability of such data and information will assist in quantifying the relationship between air pollution and physical and mental health.
- Undertake analytical work to investigate issues such as the association between air pollution and COVID-19, substantiate the nexus between climate change and air pollution, analyze the effects of preexisting health conditions that can be exacerbated due to exposure, and explore the effect of immunization such as pneumococcal vaccines among children in reducing morbidity precipitated by air pollution.
- Set up mechanisms to make available research grants and/or innovation funds to encourage technical work.

NOTES

1. Measured using annual average $PM_{2.5}$ concentration.
2. Stroke, ischemic heart disease, chronic obstructive pulmonary disease, and lower respiratory tract infection (IHME 2019).

REFERENCES

HEI (Health Effects Institute). 2020. *State of Global Air 2020: Special Report*. Boston, MA: Health Effects Institute.

IHME (Institute for Health Metrics and Evaluation). 2019. "Bangladesh." Seattle: University of Washington. https://www.healthdata.org/bangladesh.

IQAir. 2021. *World Air Quality Report: Region and City PM2.5 Ranking*. Goldach: Switzerland. https://www.iqair.com/bangladesh/dhaka.

SciJinks. n.d. "How Is Air Quality Measured?" SciJinks. https://tinyurl.com/y54nx7ja.

World Bank. Forthcoming. *Building Back a Greener Bangladesh: Country Environmental Analysis*. Washington, DC: World Bank.

Detailed Review of Existing Literature Linking Air Pollution and Health

This appendix presents an analysis of the short- and long-term effects of ambient air pollution based on 85 peer-reviewed studies. This literature was scanned using PubMed and Google Scholar databases. In addition, a more targeted search was conducted of research papers and reports focusing specifically on some of the air pollutants. Additionally, to provide a complete overview, this appendix summarizes the effect of indoor air pollution on human health.

Air pollution is defined as any substance in the air that may harm humans, animals, vegetation, or materials (Kampa and Castanas 2008). Air pollutants are generated from various sources, and each pollutant can have differing characteristics depending on the composition, source, and conditions under which they were produced. Fine particulate matter (PM) is a particular cause of concern for human health, as these very small particles can penetrate deep into the lungs, enter the bloodstream, and travel to organs causing systemic damages to tissues and cells. The main pathway of exposure from air pollution is through the respiratory tract.

Short-term effects of air pollution on health are temporary and can range from discomfort, such as irritation of the eyes, nose, skin, and throat; wheezing; coughing; tightness in the chest; headache; nausea; dizziness; and breathing difficulties to more serious effects including chronic obstructive pulmonary disease (COPD), asthma, pneumonia, lung and heart problems, and high rates of hospitalization (a measure of morbidity) (Manisalidis et al. 2020). These problems can be aggravated by extended periods of long-term exposure to air pollutants. The health of susceptible individuals (such as the elderly, children, and those with preexisting health conditions) can be adversely impacted even at low exposure levels. In children, air pollution can cause reduced lung growth and function, respiratory infections, and aggravated asthma. Air pollution exposure in early human life is associated with cardiovascular, mental, and perinatal disorders, leading to infant mortality or chronic disease in adults (Manisalidis et al. 2020).

Long-term effects of air pollution on health include chronic asthma, pulmonary insufficiency, cardiovascular diseases, and cardiovascular deaths. Type 2 diabetes, systemic inflammation, and neurodegenerative conditions like Alzheimer's disease and dementia have also been linked to long-term air pollution exposure (Schraufnagel et al. 2019). The International Agency for Research on Cancer (IARC) classifies air pollution, in particular $PM_{2.5}$, as a leading cause of cancer (Bernard et al. 2001; IARC 2013).

EFFECTS OF AMBIENT AIR POLLUTION ON HEALTH: SHORT TERM

Respiratory-related problems. Epidemiological and experimental studies show an association between exposure to ambient air pollution and respiratory allergy. There is strong evidence to support an association between exposure to PM and the development of asthma (Sompornrattanaphan et al. 2020) and can exacerbate preexisting asthma (Bowatte et al. 2015). Asthma, a complex disease influenced by both environmental and genetic factors, is one of the most common chronic, noncommunicable diseases in children and adults (Papi et al. 2018). It is characterized by variable respiratory symptoms and variable airflow limitation. Several air pollutants have been found to be positively associated with increased emergency department (ED) visits in Seoul, the Republic of Korea, for example (Noh et al. 2016). The air pollutants studied included carbon monoxide (CO), nitrogen dioxide (NO_2), ozone (O_3), sulfur dioxide (SO_2), and PM_{10}. The strongest association was a 9.6 percent increase in the risk of ED visits for asthma per interquartile range (IQR) increase in O_3 concentration. IQR changes in NO_2 and PM_{10} concentrations were also significantly associated with ED visits. Rahman et al. (2022) explored respiratory ED visit associations with exposures to $PM_{2.5}$ in Dhaka city, Bangladesh, and found a significant association between $PM_{2.5}$ with increased respiratory ED visits up to 0.84 percent of ED visits per 10 micrograms per cubic meter ($\mu g/m^3$) increase of exposure to $PM_{2.5}$. The health effect varied with season, the highest being during monsoon season, when fossil-fuel combustion sources dominated exposures (Rahman et al. 2022).

Acute lower respiratory infection (ALRI), which comprises pneumonia and bronchiolitis, is the largest single cause of mortality among young children worldwide and is responsible for a substantial burden of disease among young children in developing countries. In Ho Chi Minh City, Vietnam, the short-term effects of daily average exposure to air pollutants on hospital admissions of children less than 5 years of age for ALRI were assessed (Le et al. 2012). In the dry season, risks for ALRI hospital admissions with average pollutant lag (one to six days) were highest for NO_2 and SO_2 in the single-pollutant case-crossover analyses, with excess risks of 8.50 percent and 5.85 percent observed, respectively. The results support the presence of an association between air pollution and increased ALRI admissions. A systematic review and meta-analysis showed a positive association between daily levels of ambient air pollution markers and hospitalization of children due to pneumonia (Nhung et al. 2017). $PM_{2.5}$ has been linked to adverse respiratory outcomes in children. Sherris et al. (2021) analyzed data from health surveillance of children less than 5 years of age between 2005 and 2014 in one neighborhood of Dhaka, Bangladesh, including daily physician-confirmed diagnoses of pneumonia and upper respiratory infection. It was found that elevated ambient $PM_{2.5}$ levels were associated with an increased incidence of child pneumonia, and this relationship varied among days with different source composition of $PM_{2.5}$. COPD refers to a group of diseases that cause airflow blockage and breathing-related problems. Ambient air pollution is associated with lower lung function and increased COPD prevalence (Doiron et al. 2019).

Cardiovascular diseases (CVD) and hypertension. A study examined cardiovascular health effects of $PM_{2.5}$ exposure in Dhaka (Khan et al. 2019). A significant effect of $PM_{2.5}$ was observed two to four days after the exposure, with a 12 percent increase in CVD emergency room visits. The extent of delay was different according to the nutritional status of patients. A meta-analysis of studies in seven international and Chinese databases found that short-term exposures to air pollutants (PM_{10}, $PM_{2.5}$, SO_2, NO_2) were significantly associated with hypertension (Yang et al. 2018a). Ambient air pollution is also associated with higher hypertension prevalence and elevated blood pressure in children and adolescents (Yan et al. 2021).

Cancer. In a study conducted in Chongqing, Guangzhou, and Beijing, China, daily data on $PM_{2.5}$, PM_{10}, SO_2, O_3, and lung cancer mortality were collected to assess the short-term effect of air pollution on cancer (Wu et al. 2020). After stratification, the current-day $PM_{2.5}$, PM_{10}, and O_3 during the warm season in Beijing and $PM_{2.5}$, PM_{10}, and SO_2 during the cold season in Chongqing and Guangzhou were found to be positively associated with lung cancer mortality (excess risk ranged from 0.93 percent to 7.16 percent with each 10 $\mu g/m^3$ increment in different pollutants). Male and elderly lung cancer patients were more sensitive to the short-term effect of air pollution.

Menstrual disorders. Short-term (concurrent day and within one week prior) ambient air pollution exposure has been linked to menstrual disorders in Xi'an, a metropolis in northwestern China (Liang, Xu, Fan, et al. 2020). Data on outpatient visits between 2010 and 2016 (2,239 days) were collected and a total of 51,893 outpatient visits for menstrual disorders were recorded. A 10 $\mu g/m^3$ increase of PM_{10} and NO_2 concentrations corresponded to 0.236 percent and 2.173 percent increase in outpatient visits for menstrual disorders (at concurrent day and previous one day), respectively. The association was more significant in young females (18–29 years), and there was no obvious association observed between SO_2 and menstrual disorder outpatient visits.

Human papillomavirus (HPV) infections. HPV infections are common sexually transmitted diseases among reproductive-age women and are viewed with increasing concern. Short-term exposure to ambient pollutants and daily outpatient visits for HPV infections in China were assessed by Liang, Xu, Li, et al. (2020). A 10 $\mu g/m^3$ increase of PM_{10}, $PM_{2.5}$, SO_2, and NO_2 or a 0.1 mg/m^3 rise of CO in concurrent day concentrations were associated with increased risk in daily outpatient visits for HPV infections. The association was more significant in women ages 41 and older. The study concluded that short-term exposure to ambient pollutants may be associated with an increased risk of HPV infections.

Mental health effects. Daily concentrations of ambient air pollution were averaged from 19 fixed monitoring stations across three subtropical Chinese cities, and data on the morbidity of mental disorders were collected from three psychiatric specialty hospitals (Li et al. 2020). The number of daily outpatient visits for mental disorders increased with higher air pollutant ($PM_{2.5}$, PM_{10}, SO_2 and NO_2) concentrations, and the effect of NO_2 appeared to be consistently significant across the three cities. In addition, it was found that air pollution exhibited stronger effects for males and adults. The study concluded that acute exposure to air pollution, especially NO_2, might be an important trigger of mental disorders. In Xi'an, a northwestern Chinese metropolis, a 10 μg/m³ increase of SO_2 and NO_2 levels corresponded to a significant increase in the number of outpatient visits for depression on concurrent days, and this relationship appeared stronger in the cold seasons. However, the association of PM_{10} was only significant in males ages 30 to 50 on concurrent days. A hospital-based study in northwestern China (Zhou et al. 2021) found a positive association between SO_2 and NO_2 and daily outpatient visits due to anxiety (after adjusting for the day of the week and weather conditions including temperature, humidity, sunlight hours, and rainfalls) of 4.11 percent for SO_2 and 3.97 percent for NO_2.

EFFECTS OF AMBIENT AIR POLLUTION ON HEALTH: LONG TERM

Common morbidities associated with long-term exposure. Lipfert (2018) investigated the long-term association (exposure range from 60 days to 35 years) of morbidity with air pollution and cataloged them with respect to cardiovascular, respiratory, cancer, diabetes, hospitalization, neurological, and pregnancy-birth endpoints. Pollutant associations with cardiovascular indicators, lung function, respiratory symptoms, and low birth weight are more likely to be significant than with disease incidence, heart attacks, diabetes, or neurological endpoints. Carbon and $PM_{2.5}$ are most likely to be significant for cardiovascular outcomes, carbon and O_3 for respiratory outcomes, NO_2 for neurological outcomes, and PM_{10} for birth and pregnancy outcomes. Long-term exposure to low-level air pollution is associated with the development of COPD, even below current European Union (EU) and US limit values and possibly World Health Organization (WHO) guidelines, according to a large European study, where COPD incidence was 1.17 per 5 μg/m³ for $PM_{2.5}$, 1.11 per 10 μg/m³ for NO_2, and 1.11 per 0.5 μg/m³ (Liu et al. 2021).

Noncommunicable diseases. A comprehensive systematic review and meta-analysis looking at association between ambient air pollution and blood pressure showed significant associations of long-term exposures to $PM_{2.5}$ with hypertension (Yang et al. 2018). Stratified analyses showed a generally stronger relationship among studies of men, Asians, North Americans, and areas with higher air pollutant levels. Another systemic review and meta-analysis found that long-term ambient PM_{10} exposure was associated with higher hypertension prevalence and elevated blood pressure in children and adolescents. Current cumulative evidence appears to suggest that type 2 diabetes mellitus-related biomarkers increase with increasing exposure duration and concentration of air pollutants (Li et al. 2019). Long-term exposure to air pollution was also found to be associated with increased risk of diabetes in a Chinese population, particularly in individuals who were younger, overweight, or obese (Yang, Qian, Li, et al. 2018). PM_1, $PM_{2.5}$, and PM_{10} were significantly associated with increased diabetes prevalence. In a multicenter European study (ELAPSE), long-term air pollution exposure was associated with incidence of stroke and coronary heart disease, even air pollutant concentrations lower than current limit values (Wolf et al. 2021). The incidence of stroke was associated with

$PM_{2.5}$ (1.10 per 5 μg/m³ increase), NO_2 (1.08 per 10 μg/m³ increase), and black carbon (1.06 per 0.5 10⁻⁵/m increase), while coronary heart disease incidence was associated only with NO_2.

Environmental exposures may increase the risk of autoimmune diseases. Air pollution is a potential contributor to diseases such as rheumatoid arthritis and systemic lupus erythematosus. A retrospective observational study (Adami et al. 2022) concluded that long-term exposure to air pollution was associated with higher risk of developing autoimmune diseases, in particular, rheumatoid arthritis, connective tissue diseases, and inflammatory bowel diseases. Every 10 μg/m³ increase in PM_{10} concentration was associated with an incremental 7 percent risk of having autoimmune disease. Exposure to PM_{10} above 30 μg/m³ and $PM_{2.5}$ above 20 μg/m³ was associated with a 12 percent and 13 percent higher risk of autoimmune disease, respectively.

A recent pooled analysis of seven European cohorts investigated the relationship between long-term low-level air pollution exposure and lung cancer incidence (Hvidtfeldt, Severi, et al. 2021). A significantly higher risk for lung cancer with higher exposure to $PM_{2.5}$ was found with risk estimates elevated for subjects with exposure even below the EU limit value of 25 μg/m³. Another European study (ELAPSE) addressed the potential association between specific elemental components of $PM_{2.5}$ and lung cancer incidence (Hvidtfeldt, Chen, et al. 2021) and found a positive association. Chen et al. (2022) assessed the associations of bladder cancer incidence with residential exposure to pollutants in a pooled cohort and found a positive though statistically nonsignificant association between $PM_{2.5}$ and bladder cancer incidence. So et al. (2021) observed positive linear associations between liver cancer incidence and exposure to NO_2, $PM_{2.5}$, and black carbon and liver cancer incidence.

Prenatal exposure to air pollution and child stunting, wasting, and underweight. Goyal and Canning (2018) explored the relationship between exposure to ambient $PM_{2.5}$ in utero and child stunting by pooling data from the Bangladesh Demographic and Health Survey conducted between 2004 and 2014 and calculating children's exposure to ambient $PM_{2.5}$ in utero using high resolution satellite data. They found significant increases in the relative risk of child stunting, wasting, and underweight with higher levels of in utero exposure to $PM_{2.5}$. Over half of all children in the sample were exposed to ambient $PM_{2.5}$ levels exceeding 46 μg/m³ and had a relative risk of stunting of over 1.13 times that of children in the lowest quartile of exposure. While there is debate on the specific timing of exposure most relevant to child morbidity and mortality, the effects of prenatal and neonatal exposure to ambient PM levels have been found to be significant and lasting due to high sensitivity during fetal development and early life (Goldizen, Sly, and Knibbs 2018). Another study from Bangladesh investigated the differences in the associations of ambient and household $PM_{2.5}$ in the timings and magnitudes of prenatal and postnatal exposures across males and females and found that (1) the use of solid fuels was associated with respiratory illness among girls but not boys, (2) prenatal exposure to ambient $PM_{2.5}$ was associated with stunting in boys but not girls, and (3) postnatal exposure was associated with stunting in both males and females (Kurata, Takahashi, and Hibiki 2020). Psychological complications, autism, retinopathy, fetal growth, and low birth weight seem to be related to long-term exposure to air pollution as well (Manisalidis et al. 2020).

EFFECTS OF INDOOR HOUSEHOLD AIR POLLUTION ON HEALTH

According to WHO, indoor air pollution from burning of biomass fuel has emerged as one of the top 10 global threats to public health: it accounts for 2.7 percent of the global burden of disease (Alim et al. 2014). Levels of exposure are reported to be higher for women and children, who spend most time indoors during cooking. Indoor air pollution is the second largest global environmental contributor to morbidity and causes more than 5 million premature deaths from illnesses. Indoor air pollution is also associated with reduced work productivity, material damages, and increased health system expenses.

PM is a principal component of indoor air pollution in homes. PM originates from a variety of human-made and natural sources. Natural sources include pollen, spores, bacteria, plant and animal debris, and suspended crustal materials. Human-made sources consist of industrial emissions and combustion by-products from incinerators, motor vehicles, and power plants. Indoor sources include cigarette smoking, cooking, wood and other biomass burning in stoves and fireplaces, cleaning activities that resuspend dust particles (for example, sweeping), and penetration of outdoor particles into the indoor environment (Wallace et al. 2003). The contribution of indoor sources to personal exposure to $PM_{2.5}$ and ultrafine particles seems to be greater than from outdoor traffic sources. Cooking was identified as one of the major indoor activities affecting exposure to aerosols. Indoor-air-pollution-mediated health concerns mainly include mortality rates and incidences of respiratory and nonrespiratory diseases. Significant relationships between exposure to major indoor air pollutants and various short-term and long-term respiratory health outcomes such as wheezing, breathlessness, cough, phlegm, asthma, COPD, lung cancer, and, more rarely, lung function decline have been found (Bentayeb et al. 2013). The elderly (individuals over 65 years) are especially vulnerable to these effects.

Short-term effects of indoor air pollution

Studies of school-age children in Seattle found that $PM_{2.5}$ originating from indoor sources was more potent in decreasing pulmonary function than was outdoor-derived PM. A California study found significant decreases in lung function associated with indoor PM. While this study found associations between ambient PM and lung function, it found stronger associations for indoor than outdoor central site PM concentrations (McConnell et al. 2003). A longitudinal study of 150 inner-city preschool children with asthma, conducted as a part of the Johns Hopkins Center for Childhood Asthma (Baltimore Indoor Environment Study of Asthma in Kids [BIESAK] Study) investigated the impact of indoor $PM_{2.5}$ and PM_{10} on asthma morbidity (Breysse et al. 2010). The mean indoor $PM_{2.5}$ concentration in the BIESAK study was roughly twice as high as the indoor PM_{10} concentration, and the indoor PM concentrations were significantly higher than the respective average ambient measurements made over the same time period. For every 10 µg/m^3 increase in indoor $PM_{2.5-10}$ concentration, there was a 6 percent increase in the number of days of cough, wheeze, or chest tightness, after adjusting for age, race, sex, socioeconomic status, season, indoor fine PM, and ambient fine and coarse PM concentrations. In adjusted models, higher indoor coarse PM concentration was also significantly associated with increased incidence of symptoms severe enough to slow a child's activity, wheezing that limited speaking ability, nocturnal symptoms, and rescue medication use. In a panel study, children were given neurobehavioral tests following short-term (same day and up to 2 days before) and long-term exposure (365 days) to indoor $PM_{2.5}$, PM_{10}, and black carbon in school and at their residence (Saenen et al. 2016). Repeated neurobehavioral test performances of the children reflected slower Stroop Test (a measure of selective attention) and Digit-Symbol Test (visual information processing speed) performances with increasing short-term $PM_{2.5}$ exposure inside the classroom.

Burning of biomass fuel (cow dung, crop residue, dried leaves, wood, and so forth) in the kitchen releases smoke, which may impact the respiratory functions of women cooking indoors. One study showed significant association between biomass fuel use and respiratory involvement among rural women in Bangladesh (Alim et al. 2014). The prevalence of respiratory involvement (at least one among nine symptoms and two diseases) was significantly higher among biomass users than among gas users (29.9 percent versus. 11.2 percent). The biomass fuel usage elevated symptoms and diseases significantly. Akther et al. (2019) measured real-time PM_1, $PM_{2.5}$, PM_4, PM_7, PM_{10}, NO_2, and VOC from the indoor air of houses at four residential locations in Dhaka to investigate their association with lung function. A negative association between ultrafine particles and peak flow rate measurements of the residents living in these houses indicated that inhalation of ultrafine particles had a great impact on reduced lung efficiency. There was also a strong correlation between indoor and outdoor $PM_{2.5}$, suggesting indoor air was affected by outdoor air.

Long-term effects of indoor air pollution

The primary cause of COPD in women is indoor air pollution exposure, while tobacco smoking is the leading cause in men (Shetty, D'Souza, and Anand 2021). A systematic review and meta-analysis evaluated the correlation between the indoor air pollution and deaths related to COPD and COPD prevalence in South Asia from 1985 until June 2020. The results have concluded that long-term exposure to indoor pollution had a significant effect on COPD deaths as well as its symptoms. The odds ratio was in a range of 1.05 (randomized controlled trials) to 7.87 (cross-sectional studies) for all the studies mentioned. Another pooled analysis showed that exposure to indoor air pollution due to solid biomass fuels increased risk of COPD by 2.65 and chronic bronchitis by 2.89 times more compared to non-biomass fuels. Exposure to indoor air pollution is known to affect respiratory and cardiovascular health, but little is known about its effects on cognitive function. Concentrations of indoor PM arising from burning peat, wood, or coal in residential open fires were measured by Maher et al. (2021) to assess its effects on cognitive function in a sample of nearly 7,000 older people. Highest indoor $PM_{2.5}$ concentrations (60 µg/m³, that is, 2.4 times the WHO-recommended 24-hour mean) occurred when peat was burned, followed by burning of coal (30 µg/m³) and wood (17 µg/m³). The study found that exposure to PM was greater for individuals spending around five hours per day indoors with a coal-burning open fire for six months compared to those commuting via heavily trafficked roads for one hour per day for one year. After accounting for relevant confounders such as socioeconomic status, the study found a negative association between open fire usage and cognitive function as measured by cognitive tests such as word recall and verbal fluency tests. The negative association was largest and statistically strongest among women, a finding explained by the greater exposure of women to open fires in the home because they spent more time at home than men. Higher

$PM_{2.5}$ and lower ventilation rates, as assessed by carbon dioxide concentration, were associated with slower response times and reduced accuracy (fewer correct responses per minute) on the Stroop Test (a measure of selective attention) and attention deficit for 8 out 10 test metrics (Laurent et al. 2021).

REFERENCES

Adami, G., M. Pontalti, G. Cattani, M. Rossini, O. Viapiana, G. Orsolini, et al. 2022. "Association between Long-Term Exposure to Air Pollution and Immune-Mediated Diseases: A Population-Based Cohort Study." *RMD Open* 8 (1): e002055. https://doi.org/10.1136/rmdopen-2021-002055.

Akther, T., M. Ahmed, M. Shohel, F. Khanom, and A. Salam. 2019. "Particulate Matters and Gaseous Pollutants in Indoor Environment and Association of Ultra-Fine Particulate Matters (PM_1) with Lung Function." *Environmental Science and Pollution Research* 26: 5475–84. https://link.springer.com/article/10.1007/s11356-018-4043-2.

Alim, M.A., M. A. B. Sarker, S. Selim, Md. Karim, Y. Yoshida, and N. Hamajima. 2014. "Respiratory Involvements among Women Exposed to the Smoke of Traditional Biomass Fuel and Gas Fuel in a District of Bangladesh." *Environmental Health and Preventive Medicine* 19: 126–34. https://link.springer.com/article/10.1007/s12199-013-0364-4.

Bentayeb, M., M. Simoni, D. Norback, S. Baldacci, S. Maio, G. Viegi, and I. Annesi-Maesano. 2013. "Indoor Air Pollution and Respiratory Health in the Elderly." *Journal of Environmental Science and Health:* Part A, *Toxic/hazardous Substances and Environmental Engineering* 48 (14): 1783–89. https://doi.org/10.1080/10934529.2013.826052.

Bernard, S. M., J. M. Samet, A. Grambsch, K. L. Ebi, and I. Romieu. 2001. "The Potential Impacts of Climate Variability and Change on Air Pollution-Related Health Effects in the United States." *Environmental Health Perspectives* 109 (supp 2). https://ehp.niehs.nih.gov/doi/abs/10.1289/ehp.109-1240667.

Bowatte, G., C. Lodge, A. J. Lowe, B. Erbas, J. Perret, M. J. Abramson, et al. 2015. "The Influence of Childhood Traffic-Related Air Pollution Exposure on Asthma, Allergy, and Sensitization: A Systematic Review and a Meta-Analysis of Birth Cohort Studies." *Allergy* 70 (3): 245–56.

Breysse, P. N., G. B. Diette, E. C. Matsui, A. M. Butz, N. N. Hansel, and M. C. McCormack. 2010. "Indoor Air Pollution and Asthma in Children." *Proceedings of the American Thoracic Society* 7 (2):102–06. https://doi.org/10.1513/pats.200908-083RM. PMID: 20427579; PMCID: PMC3266016.

Chen, J., S. Rodopoulou, M. Strak, K. de Hoogh, T. Taj, A. H. Poulsen, et al. 2022. "Long-Term Exposure to Ambient Air Pollution and Bladder Cancer Incidence in a Pooled European Cohort: The ELAPSE Project." *British Journal of Cancer* 126 (10): 1499–507. https://doi.org/10.1038/s41416-022-01735-4.

Doiron, D., K. de Hoogh, N. Probst-Hensch, I. Fortier, Y. Cai, S. De Matteis, and A. L. Hansell. 2019. "Air Pollution, Lung Function and COPD: Results from the Population-Based UK Biobank Study." *European Respiratory Journal* 54 (1): 1802140. https://doi.org/10.1183/13993003.02140-2018.

Goldizen, F.C., P. D. Sly, and L. D. Knibbs. 2018. "Respiratory Effects of Air Pollution on Children." *Pediatric Pulmonology* 51: 94–108.

Goyal, N., and D. Canning. 2018. "Exposure to Ambient Fine Particulate Air Pollution in Utero as a Risk Factor for Child Stunting in Bangladesh." *International Journal of Environmental Research and Public Health* 15 (1): 22.

Hvidtfeldt, U. A., J. Chen, Z. J. Andersen, R. Atkinson, M. Bauwelinck, T. Bellander, et al. 2021. "Long-Term Exposure to Fine Particle Elemental Components and Lung Cancer Incidence in the ELAPSE Pooled Cohort." *Environmental Research* 193: 110568. https://doi.org/10.1016/j.envres.2020.110568.

Hvidtfeldt, U. A., G. Severi, Z. J. Andersen, R. Atkinson, M. Bauwelinck, T. Bellander, et al. 2021. "Long-Term Low-Level Ambient Air Pollution Exposure and Risk of Lung Cancer: A Pooled Analysis of 7 European Cohorts." *Environment International* 146: 106249. https://doi.org/10.1016/j.envint.2020.106249.

IARC (International Agency for Research on Cancer). 2013. "Outdoor Air Pollution a Leading Environmental Cause of Cancer Deaths." Press Release 221, October 17, 2013. https://www.iarc.who.int/news-events/iarc-outdoor-air-pollution-a-leading-environmental-cause-of-cancer-deaths.

Kampa, M., and E. Castanas. 2008. "Human Health Effects of Air Pollution." *Environmental Pollution* 151 (2): 362–67. https://doi.org/10.1016/j.envpol.2007.06.012.

Khan, R., S. Konishi, C. Fook, S. Ng, M. Umezaki, A. F. Kabir, S. Tamsin, and C. Watanabe. 2019. "Association between Short-Term Exposure to Fine Particulate Matter and Daily Emergency Room Visits at a Cardiovascular Hospital in Dhaka, Bangladesh." *Science of the Total Environment* 646: 1030–36. https://www.sciencedirect.com/science/article/abs/pii/S0048969718327840.

Kurata, M., K. Takahashi, and A. Hibiki. 2020. "Gender Differences in Associations of Household and Ambient Air Pollution with Child Health: Evidence from Household and Satellite-Based Data in Bangladesh." *World Development* 128 (April): 104779. https://www.sciencedirect.com/science/article/pii/S0305750X19304280.

Laurent, J. G. C., P. MacNaughton, E. Jones, A. S. Young, M. Bliss, S. Flanigan, et al. 2021. "Associations between Acute Exposures to $PM_{2.5}$ and Carbon Dioxide Indoors and Cognitive Function in Office Workers: A Multicountry Longitudinal Prospective Observational Study." *Environmental Research Letters* 16 (9): 094047. https://doi.org/10.1088/1748-9326/ac1bd8.

Le, T. G., L. Ngo, S. Mehta, V. D. Do, T. Q. Thach, X. D. Vu, D. T. Nguyen, and A. Cohen. 2012. "Effects of Short-Term Exposure to Air Pollution on Hospital Admissions of Young Children for Acute Lower Respiratory Infections in Ho Chi Minh City, Vietnam." *Research Reports: Health Effects Institute* (169): 5–72. PMID: 22849236.

Li, Y., L. Xu, Z. Shan, W. Teng, and C. Han. 2019. "Association between Air Pollution and Type 2 Diabetes: An Updated Review of the Literature." *Therapeutic Advances in Endocrinology and Metabolim* 10: 2042018819897046. https://doi.org/10.1177/2042018819897046.

Li, H., S. Zhang, Z. M. Qian, X. H. Xie, Y. Luo, R. Han, et al. 2020. "Short-Term Effects of Air Pollution on Cause-Specific Mental Disorders in Three Subtropical Chinese Cities." *Environmental Research* 191: 110214. https://pubmed.ncbi.nlm.nih.gov/32946889.

Liang, Z., C. Xu, Y. N. Fan, Z. Q. Liang, H. D. Kan, R. J. Chen, et al. 2020. "Association between Air Pollution and Menstrual Disorder Outpatient Visits: A Time-Series Analysis." *Ecotoxicology and Environmental Safety* 192: 110283. https://doi.org/10.1016/j.ecoenv.2020.110283.

Liang, Z., C. Xu, A. L Ji, S. Liang, H. D. Kan, R. J. Chen, et al. 2020. "Effects of Short-Term Ambient Air Pollution Exposure on HPV Infections: A Five-Year Hospital-Based Study." *Chemosphere* 252: 126615. https://doi.org/10.1016/j.chemosphere.2020.126615.

Lipfert, F.W. 2018. "Long-Term Associations of Morbidity with Air Pollution: A Catalog and Synthesis." *Journal of the Air and Waste Management Association* 68 (1): 12–28. https://doi.org/10.1080/10962247.2017.1349010.

Liu, S., J. T. Jørgensen, P. Ljungman, G. Pershagen, T. Bellander, K. Leander, et al. 2021. "Long-Term Exposure to Low-Level Air Pollution and Incidence of Chronic Obstructive Pulmonary Disease: The ELAPSE PROJECT." *Environment International* 146: 106267. https://doi.org/10.1016/j.envint.2020.106267.

Maher, B. A., V. O'Sullivan, J. Feeney, T. Gonet, and R. Anne Kenny. 2021. "Indoor Particulate Air Pollution from Open Fires and the Cognitive Function of Older People." *Environmental Research* 192: 110298. https://pubmed.ncbi.nlm.nih.gov/33039528/.

Manisalidis, I., E. Stavropoulou, A. Stavropoulos, and E. Bezirtzoglou. 2020. "Environmental and Health Impacts of Air Pollution: A Review." *Frontiers of Public Health* 8 (14). https://doi.org/10.3389/fpubh.2020.00014.

McConnell, R., K. Berhane, F. Gilliland, J. Molitor, D. Thomas, F. Lurmann, et al. 2003. "Prospective Study of Air Pollution and Bronchitic Symptoms in Children with Asthma." *American Journal of Respiratory Critical Care Medicine* 168: 790–97.

Nhung, N. T. T., H. Amini, C. Schindler, M. K. Joss, T. M. Dien, N. Probst-Hensch, L. Perez, and N. Künzli. 2017. "Short-Term Association between Ambient Air Pollution and Pneumonia in Children: A Systematic Review and Meta-Analysis of Time-Series and Case-Crossover Studies." *Environmental Pollution* 230: 1000–1008. https://doi.org/10.1016/j.envpol.2017.07.063.

Noh, J., J. Sohn, J. Cho, S. K. Cho, Y. J. Choi, C. Kim, and D. C. Shin. 2016. "Short-term Effects of Ambient Air Pollution on Emergency Department Visits for Asthma: An Assessment of Effect Modification by Prior Allergic Disease History." *Journal of Preventive Medicine and Public Health* 49 (5): 329–41. https://doi.org/10.3961/jpmph.16.038.

Papi, A., C. Brightling, S. E. Pedersen, and H. K. Reddel. 2018. "Asthma." *Lancet* 391(10122): 783–800. https://doi.org/10.1016/S0140-6736(17)33311-1.

Rahman, M. M., K. Nahar, B. A. Begum, P. K. Hopke, and G. D. Thurston. 2022. "Respiratory Emergency Department Visit Associations with Exposures to Fine Particulate Matter Mass, Constituents, and Sources in Dhaka, Bangladesh Air Pollution." *Annals of the American Thoracic Society* 19 (1): 28–38. https://doi.org/10.1513/AnnalsATS.202103-252OC.

Saenen, N. D., E. B. Provost, M. K. Viaene, C. Vanpoucke, W. Lefebvre, K. Vrijens, H. A. Roels, and T. S. Nawrot. 2016. "Recent versus Chronic Exposure to Particulate Matter Air Pollution in Association with Neurobehavioral Performance in a Panel Study of Primary Schoolchildren." *Environment International* 95 (October): 112–19. https://doi.org/10.1016/j.envint.2016.07.014.

Schraufnagel, D. E., J. R. Balmes, C. T. Cowl, S. De Matteis, S.-H. Jung, K. Mortimer, R. Perez-Padilla, et al. 2019. "Air Pollution and Noncommunicable Diseases: A Review by the Forum of International Respiratory Societies' Environmental Committee," part 2: "Air Pollution and Organ Systems." *Chest* 155 (2): 417–26. https://doi.org/10.1016/j.chest.2018.10.041.

Sherris, A. R., B. A. Begum, M. Baiocchi, D. Goswami, P. K. Hopke, W. A. Brooks, and S. P. Luby. 2021. "Associations between Ambient Fine Particulate Matter and Child Respiratory Infection: The Role of Particulate Matter Source Composition in Dhaka, Bangladesh." *Environmental Pollution* 290: 118073. https://doi.org/10.1016/j.envpol.2021.

Shetty, B. S. P., G. D'Souza, and M. Padukudru Anand. 2021. "Effect of Indoor Air Pollution on Chronic Obstructive Pulmonary Disease (COPD) Deaths in Southern Asia-A Systematic Review and Meta-Analysis." *Toxics* 9 (4): 85. https://doi.org/10.3390/toxics9040085.

So, R., J. Chen, A. J. Mehta, S. Liu, M. Strak, K. Wolf, et al. 2021. "Long-Term Exposure to Air Pollution and Liver Cancer Incidence in Six European Cohorts." *International Journal of Cancer* 149 (11): 1887–97. https://doi.org/10.1002/ijc.33743.

Sompornrattanaphan, M., T. Thongngarm, P. Ratanawatkul, C. Wongsa, and J. J. Swigris. 2020. "The Contribution of Particulate Matter to Respiratory Allergy." *Asian Pacific Journal of Allergy and Immunology* 38 (1): 19–28. http://doi.org/10.12932/AP-100619-0579.

Wallace, L. A., H. Mitchell, G. T. O'Connor, L. Neas, M. Lippmann, M. Kattan, et al. 2003. "Particle Concentrations in Inner-City Homes of Children with Asthma: The Effect of Smoking, Cooking, and Outdoor Pollution." *Environmental Health Perspectives* 111: 1265–72. https://doi.org/10.1289/ehp.6135.

Wolf, K., B. Hoffmann, Z. J. Andersen, R. W. Atkinson, M. Bauwelinck, T. Bellander, et al. 2021. "Long-Term Exposure to Low-Level Ambient Air Pollution and Incidence of Stroke and Coronary Heart Disease: A Pooled Analysis of Six European Cohorts within the ELAPSE Project." *Lancet Planet Health* 5 (9): e620-e632.

Wu, Y., R. Li, L. Cui, Y. Meng, H. Cheng, and H. Fu. 2020. "The High-Resolution Estimation of Sulfur Dioxide (SO_2) Concentration, Health Effects, and Monetary Costs in Beijing." *Chemosphere* 241: 125031. ISSN 0045-6535. https://www.sciencedirect.com/science/article/abs/pii/S0045653519322702.

Yan, M., J. Xu, C. Li, P. Guo, X. Yang, and N. J. Tang. 2021. "Associations between Ambient Air Pollutants and Blood Pressure among Children and Adolescents: A Systemic Review and Meta-Analysis." *Science of the Total Environment* 785: 147279. https://doi.org/10.1016/j.scitotenv.2021.147279.

Yang, B. Y., Z. M. Qian, S. W. Howard, M. G. Vaughn, S. J. Fan, K. K. Liu, and G. H. Dong. 2018. "Global Association between Ambient Air Pollution and Blood Pressure: A Systematic Review and Meta-Analysis." *Environmental Pollution* 235: 576–88. https://doi.org/10.1016/j.envpol.2018.01.001.

Zhou, Y. M., F. N. Fan, C. Y. Yao, C. Xu, X. L. Liu, X. Li, et al. 2021 "Association between Short-Term Ambient Air Pollution and Outpatient Visits of Anxiety: A Hospital-Based Study in Northwestern China." *Environmental Research* 197: 111071. https://doi.org/10.1016/j.envres.2021.111071.

Tables, Figures, and Map

TABLE B.1 Distribution of the sample, by study site

RESPONDENT TYPE	PERSISTENT TRAFFIC	MAJOR CONSTRUCTION AND TRAFFIC	BRICK KILNS	COMPARATOR	TOTAL
In households with children (<10 years)	1,238 (253)	1,157 (255)	1,198 (254)	1,377 (251)	4,970
In households with elderly population (65+ years)	487 (94)	424 (83)	502 (100)	577 (98)	1,990
In mixed households	1,295 (280)	1,309 (288)	1,214 (272)	1,472 (276)	5,290
Total	3,020 (627)	2,890 (626)	2,914 (626)	3,426 (625)	12,250

Source: Original compilation for this publication. World Bank.
Note: The table shows the number of individuals from household types by location. Numbers of households are in parentheses.

TABLE B.2 Scoring mechanism to assess the likelihood of a lower respiratory tract infection

SERIAL NUMBER	QUESTION	SCORE (IF YES)
1	Did you suffer from a cough in the past 14 days?	2
1a	Is/was your cough productive (with sputum)?	2
1b	Is the sputum thick/heavy?	1
1c	Was the sputum unclear (rusty/green/yellow)?	1
1d	Did you expel any blood with the cough?	2
2	Have you experienced any shortness of breath or heaviness in the chest in the past 14 days?	2
2a	Is/was your breathing accompanied with a wheezing sound?	3
Scoring restricted to individuals who have responded positively to experiencing a cough or breathing problem (question 1 or 2)		
3	Was your cough or breathing problem accompanied by a fever?	1
3a	Did you experience chills with the fever?	1
3b	Did the fever last for more than 5 days?	1
4	Did you experience any body aches or weakness along with the cough or breathing problem?	1

Source: World Bank.
Note: The table shows the set of questions used to predict the likelihood of a respondent experiencing a respiratory infection using a 14-day recall. Individuals with a score of six or above are considered to have a strong likelihood of experiencing or having experienced a respiratory infection.

TABLE B.3 **Means tests of exposure to pollutants, by location**

	PERSISTENT TRAFFIC VERSUS COMPARATOR	MAJOR CONSTRUCTION AND TRAFFIC VERSUS COMPARATOR	BRICK KILNS VERSUS COMPARATOR	PERSISTENT TRAFFIC VERSUS BRICK KILNS	MAJOR CONSTRUCTION AND TRAFFIC VERSUS BRICK KILNS
			See figure 3.1		
PM_1 (μg/m³)	*	..	***	***	***
$PM_{2.5}$ (μg/m³)	***	***	***	**	***
PM_{10} (μg/m³)	***	***	**	***	***
NO_2 (ppb)	***	***	**	***	***
VOC (ppb)	***	***	***	..	..
			See figure 3.2		
$PM_{2.5}$ (μg/m³)	***	***	***	**	***
PM_{10} (μg/m³)	***	***	**	***	***

Source: World Bank.
Note: Test statistics are derived using standard t-tests. PM = particulate matter. PM numbers indicate the size of particles: PM_1 indicates particles of 1 micrometer, and so forth. NO_2 = nitrogen dioxide. ppb = parts per billion. μg/m³ = micrograms per cubic meter. VOC = volatile organic compound.
***, **, and * represent significance below the 1 percent, 5 percent, and 10 percent levels.

TABLE B.4 **Prevalence of cough and breathing difficulties**

	MEAN (%)
Productive cough	42.9
Expelled thick sputum	56.8
Color of sputum (of individuals with thick sputum)	
Clear	71.8
Rusty	7.7
Green	3.0
Yellow	17.5
Blood with cough	2.5
Breathing difficulty with wheezing sounds	56.5

Source: World Bank.
Note: The proportions presented on the table's dimensions are restricted to individuals who reported experiencing a cough or breathing difficulties in the 14 days preceding the survey.

TABLE B.5 **Means tests of short-term illnesses, by location, demographic characteristics, and socioeconomic status**

	PERSISTENT TRAFFIC VERSUS COMPARATOR	MAJOR CONSTRUCTION AND TRAFFIC VERSUS COMPARATOR	BRICK KILNS VERSUS COMPARATOR	PERSISTENT TRAFFIC VERSUS BRICK KILNS	MAJOR CONSTRUCTION AND TRAFFIC VERSUS BRICK KILNS
			See figure 3.4		
Cough	..	..	**	***	..
Breathing difficulties	**	***	***	..	*
Fever	***	***	***	***	***
Body aches	..	*	***	***	***
General weakness	***	**	*	..	..
Eye issues	..	..	***	**	***
Throat issues	***	..	..	***	..

continued

TABLE B.5, *continued*

	PERSISTENT TRAFFIC VERSUS COMPARATOR	MAJOR CONSTRUCTION AND TRAFFIC VERSUS COMPARATOR	BRICK KILNS VERSUS COMPARATOR	PERSISTENT TRAFFIC VERSUS BRICK KILNS	MAJOR CONSTRUCTION AND TRAFFIC VERSUS BRICK KILNS
Nose issues	*	..	***	***	***
Skin issues	***	***	***	***	**

	See figure 3.5			See figure 3.6	
	0–5 YEARS VERSUS 6–19 YEARS	**0–5 YEARS VERSUS 20–64 YEARS**	**0–5 YEARS VERSUS 65+ YEARS**	**MALE VERSUS FEMALE**	
Cough	***	***	***	..	
Breathing difficulties	***	..	***	..	
Fever	***	***	..	***	
Eye issues	..	***	***	***	
Nose issues	***	***	***	***	
Skin issues	***	***	***	***	
Throat issues	***	***	***	***	

	See figure 3.7			
	POOREST VERSUS POOR	**POOREST VERSUS MID**	**POOREST VERSUS RICH**	**POOREST VERSUS RICHEST**
Cough	***	*	..	***
Breathing difficulties	..	..	..	..
Fever	**	***	..	..
Eye issues	**	..	..	..
Nose issues	..	..	..	**
Skin issues	**	..	..	***
Throat issues	*	..	..	**

Source: World Bank.
Note: Test statistics are derived using standard *t*-tests.
***, **, and * represent significance below the 1 percent, 5 percent, and 10 percent levels.

TABLE B.6 **Means tests of proportion of individuals with respiratory infections, by location and demographic characteristics**

PERSISTENT TRAFFIC VERSUS COMPARATOR	MAJOR CONSTRUCTION AND TRAFFIC VERSUS COMPARATOR	BRICK KILNS VERSUS COMPARATOR	PERSISTENT TRAFFIC VERSUS BRICK KILNS	MAJOR CONSTRUCTION AND TRAFFIC VERSUS BRICK KILNS
See figure 3.8				
***	..	*	***	..

0–5 YEARS VERSUS 6–19 YEARS	0–5 YEARS VERSUS 20–64 YEARS	0–5 YEARS VERSUS 65+ YEARS	MALE VERSUS FEMALE
See figure 3.9			
***	..	***	*

Source: World Bank.
Note: The table presents the proportion of individuals who scored at least 5 in the Respiratory Infection Score, suggesting a likely presence of a respiratory infection but not substantiated by radiological tests and, hence, not clinically proven. Test statistics are derived using standard *t*-tests.
***, **, and * represent significance below the 1 percent, 5 percent, and 10 percent levels.

TABLE B.7 Means tests of NCDs by location, demographic characteristics, and socioeconomic status

	PERSISTENT TRAFFIC VERSUS COMPARATOR	MAJOR CONSTRUCTION AND TRAFFIC VERSUS COMPARATOR	BRICK KILNS VERSUS COMPARATOR	PERSISTENT TRAFFIC VERSUS BRICK KILNS	MAJOR CONSTRUCTION AND TRAFFIC VERSUS BRICK KILNS
			See figure 3.12		
Allergies	..	***	***	***	*
Diabetes	..	*	..	..	..
Heart disease	..	..	..	..	..
Hypertension	***	***	***	..	**
History of stroke	..	..	**	..	..
Chronic respiratory illnesses	***	*	..	**	..

	See figure 3.13			See figure 3.14	
	0–5 YEARS VERSUS 6–19 YEARS	**0–5 YEARS VERSUS 20–64 YEARS**	**0–5 YEARS VERSUS 65+ YEARS**	**MALE VERSUS FEMALE**	
Allergies	***	***	***	***	
Diabetes	..	***	***	***	
Heart disease	**	***	***	..	
Hypertension	..	***	***	***	
History of stroke	..	***	***	***	
Chronic respiratory illnesses	..	***	***	..	

	POOREST VERSUS POOR	POOREST VERSUS MID	POOREST VERSUS RICH	POOREST VERSUS RICHEST
		See figure 3.15		
Allergies	..	*	***	***
Diabetes	..	..	***	***
Heart disease	..	..	..	***
Hypertension	..	***	***	***
History of stroke	..	..	..	*
Chronic respiratory illnesses	..	*	..	..

Source: World Bank.
Note: Test statistics are derived using standard *t*-tests. NCD = noncommunicable disease.
***, **, and * represent significance below the 1 percent, 5 percent, and 10 percent levels.

TABLE B.8 Correlates of having a productive cough, breathing difficulties, and likely respiratory infection (14-day recall)

	PRODUCTIVE COUGH		BREATHING DIFFICULTIES		LOWER RESPIRATORY TRACT INFECTION	
	ADJUSTED ODDS RATIOS	STANDARD ERROR	ADJUSTED ODDS RATIOS	STANDARD ERROR	ADJUSTED ODDS RATIOS	STANDARD ERROR
Base: Comparator						
Persistent traffic	0.806	1.48	1.411**	2.00	0.748**	2.52
Major construction and traffic	0.996	0.03	1.651***	2.94	0.929	0.66
Brick kilns	1.027	0.22	1.177	1.05	0.943	0.61
$PM_{2.5}$	1.125**	2.08	1.128*	1.72	1.081*	1.71
PM_{10}	1.005	0.08	1.066	1.02	1.033	0.69
Base: Age 20–64 years						

continued

TABLE B.8, *continued*

	PRODUCTIVE COUGH		BREATHING DIFFICULTIES		LOWER RESPIRATORY TRACT INFECTION	
	ADJUSTED ODDS RATIOS	**STANDARD ERROR**	**ADJUSTED ODDS RATIOS**	**STANDARD ERROR**	**ADJUSTED ODDS RATIOS**	**STANDARD ERROR**
0–5 years	1.597*	1.94	1.703*	1.70	1.979***	3.67
6–19 years	0.738	1.59	0.659*	1.73	0.836	1.28
65+ years	2.699***	6.71	2.970***	6.98	2.304***	6.71
Male	0.883	1.25	1.107	0.80	0.891	1.42
Base: Outdoor low-skilled work						
None (Children < 5 years)	0.879	0.48	0.661	1.22	0.533***	3.11
Indoor low-skilled work	0.870	0.62	0.653	1.62	0.726*	1.88
indoor skilled work	0.854	0.70	0.710	1.32	0.641***	2.62
Homemaker	0.854	0.78	0.831	0.79	0.697**	2.38
Student	0.654	1.45	0.620	1.30	0.483***	3.22
Other	0.786	1.11	0.687	1.59	0.645***	2.71
Household size	0.951*	1.81	0.977	0.64	0.946**	2.40
Improved source of fuel	1.005	0.05	0.858	1.24	0.988	0.15
Hours spent outdoors	1.023**	2.29	1.015	1.20	1.015*	1.81
Base: Poorest						
Poor	0.749**	2.18	0.656***	2.66	0.746***	2.87
Mid	0.736**	2.26	0.791	1.58	0.745***	2.81
Rich	1.055	0.42	0.674**	2.47	0.827*	1.83
Richest	1.150	1.04	0.912	0.57	0.942	0.56
Allergies	2.881***	12.03	3.504***	12.24	2.714***	13.83
Diabetes	1.663***	3.07	1.774***	3.14	1.627***	3.49
Hypertension	0.991	0.06	1.232	1.31	1.109	0.88
Heart disease	1.631**	2.40	3.376***	6.26	1.736***	3.24
Stroke	1.764**	1.99	1.130	0.38	1.682**	2.10
Pseudo R²	0.07		0.11		0.06	
N	12,190		12,190		12,190	

Source: World Bank.
Note: The table shows adjusted odds ratios (AORs) from a logistic model. The binary dependent variable is whether a respondent has reported experiencing a productive cough with a thick sputum had breathing difficulties and had a likely respiratory infection in the 14 days preceding the survey. Robust standard errors are calculated using the Huber-White (1967) approach. Results are interpretable as percentage changes ([AOR – 1] * 100 = percentage change). PM = particulate matter. PM numbers indicate the size of the particles: PM_1 indicates particles of 1 micrometer, and so forth.
***, **, and * represent significance below the 1 percent, 5 percent, and 10 percent levels.

TABLE B.9 **Heterogeneity analysis: productive cough (14-day recall)**

	PERSISTENT TRAFFIC VERSUS COMPARATOR		MAJOR CONSTRUCTION AND TRAFFIC VERSUS COMPARATOR		BRICK KILNS VERSUS COMPARATOR		PERSISTENT TRAFFIC VERSUS MAJOR CONSTRUCTION AND TRAFFIC		BRICK KILNS VERSUS MAJOR CONSTRUCTION AND TRAFFIC	
	ADJUSTED ODDS RATIOS	STANDARD ERROR	ADJUSTED ODDS RATIOS	STANDARD ERROR	ADJUSTED ODDS RATIOS	STANDARD ERROR	ADJUSTED ODDS RATIOS	STANDARD ERROR	ADJUSTED ODDS RATIOS	STANDARD ERROR
Demographics										
0–5 years	1.263	0.62	1.883*	1.82	0.994	0.02	0.670	1.13	0.526**	2.00
6–19 years	1.038	0.12	1.415	1.19	0.830	0.65	0.719	1.06	0.579*	1.87
65+ years	0.919	0.21	0.745	0.76	0.605	1.41	1.219	0.44	0.799	0.56
Male	0.819	0.84	1.005	0.02	1.230	0.97	0.806	0.90	1.230	0.95
Household size	1.054	0.65	1.211***	2.70	1.197**	2.30	0.882	1.41	0.990	0.12
Comorbidities										
Allergies	0.854	0.59	1.200	0.75	0.723	1.38	0.726	1.19	0.603**	2.15
Diabetes	0.859	0.31	0.912	0.20	0.522	1.44	0.952	0.10	0.594	1.09
Hypertension	1.228	0.47	1.201	0.44	1.198	0.47	1.051	0.10	1.010	0.02
Heart disease	0.269	1.64	1.064	0.12	1.100	0.18	0.249*	1.75	1.030	0.06
Stroke	2.649	1.08	7.028**	2.39	0.681	0.39	0.377	1.26	0.090***	2.72
Pseudo R²	0.07						0.07			
N	12,190						8,782			

Source: World Bank.

Note: The table shows adjusted odds ratios (AORs) from a logistic model. The binary dependent variable is whether a respondent has reported experiencing a productive cough with a thick sputum in the 14 days preceding the survey. Analysis of heterogeneity across study sites is reported for selected demographic characteristics and comorbidities with the comparator site and major construction and persistent traffic as the base category. Results are restricted to persistent traffic, major construction and traffic, and brick kiln sites. Robust standard errors are calculated using the Huber-White (1967) approach methods. Results are also interpretable as percentage changes ([AOR − 1] * 100 = percentage change).

***, **, and * represent significance below the 1 percent, 5 percent, and 10 percent levels.

TABLE B.10 Heterogeneity analysis: breathing difficulties (14-day recall)

	PERSISTENT TRAFFIC VERSUS COMPARATOR		MAJOR CONSTRUCTION AND TRAFFIC VERSUS COMPARATOR		BRICK KILNS VERSUS COMPARATOR		PERSISTENT TRAFFIC VERSUS MAJOR CONSTRUCTION AND TRAFFIC		BRICK KILNS VERSUS MAJOR CONSTRUCTION AND TRAFFIC	
	ADJUSTED ODDS RATIOS	STANDARD ERROR	ADJUSTED ODDS RATIOS	STANDARD ERROR	ADJUSTED ODDS RATIOS	STANDARD ERROR	ADJUSTED ODDS RATIOS	STANDARD ERROR	ADJUSTED ODDS RATIOS	STANDARD ERROR
Demographics										
0–5 years	1.212	0.35	3.320**	2.35	1.870	1.15	0.363**	2.42	0.561	1.44
6–19 years	0.760	0.64	1.225	0.49	1.258	0.55	0.620	1.24	1.019	0.05
65+ years	0.543	1.36	0.539	1.48	0.397**	2.13	1.012	0.03	0.742	0.66
Male	0.600*	1.76	0.861	0.53	0.863	0.50	0.690	1.40	1.009	0.04
Household size	0.773**	2.43	1.150	1.50	1.028	0.25	0.673***	3.87	0.896	1.02
Comorbidities										
Allergies	1.647	1.56	2.279***	2.67	1.317	0.86	0.730	1.12	0.578*	1.95
Diabetes	0.872	0.25	1.092	0.18	0.522	1.25	0.789	0.43	0.476	1.45
Hypertension	0.762	0.54	1.399	0.75	1.572	1.06	0.545	1.18	1.109	0.23
Heart disease	0.449	1.30	0.603	0.91	1.225	0.39	0.740	0.49	2.043	1.36
Stroke	0.617	0.49	1.301	0.31	0.602	0.49	0.483	0.79	0.458	0.79
Pseudo R²	0.11						0.11			
N	12,190						8,776			

Source: World Bank.

Note: The table shows adjusted odds ratios (AORs) from a logistic model. The binary dependent variable is whether a respondent has reported experiencing breathing problems in the 14 days preceding the survey. Analysis of heterogeneity across study sites is reported for selected demographic characteristics and comorbidities with the comparator site and major construction and persistent traffic as the base category. Results are restricted to persistent traffic, major construction and traffic, and brick kiln sites. Robust standard errors are calculated using the Huber-White (1967) approach methods. Results are also interpretable as percentage changes ([AOR − 1] * 100 = percentage change).

***, **, and * represent significance below the 1 percent, 5 percent, and 10 percent levels.

TABLE B.11 Heterogeneity analysis: lower respiratory tract infection (14-day recall)

	PERSISTENT TRAFFIC VERSUS COMPARATOR		MAJOR CONSTRUCTION AND TRAFFIC VERSUS COMPARATOR		BRICK KILNS VERSUS COMPARATOR		PERSISTENT TRAFFIC VERSUS MAJOR CONSTRUCTION AND TRAFFIC		BRICK KILNS VERSUS MAJOR CONSTRUCTION AND TRAFFIC	
	ADJUSTED ODDS RATIOS	STANDARD ERROR	ADJUSTED ODDS RATIOS	STANDARD ERROR	ADJUSTED ODDS RATIOS	STANDARD ERROR	ADJUSTED ODDS RATIOS	STANDARD ERROR	ADJUSTED ODDS RATIOS	STANDARD ERROR
Demographics										
0–5 years	1.446	1.21	2.326***	3.06	1.220	0.70	0.621*	1.68	0.521**	2.49
6–19 years	1.032	0.13	1.280	1.06	1.029	0.13	0.796	0.91	0.792	0.99
65+ years	1.139	0.39	1.067	0.20	0.677	1.24	1.063	0.17	0.618	1.39
Male	0.873	0.72	1.048	0.27	1.211	1.10	0.828	0.99	1.154	0.80
Household size	1.020	0.30	1.229***	3.48	1.184**	2.55	0.841**	2.43	0.963	0.53
Comorbidities										
Allergies	1.184	0.79	1.416*	1.75	0.999	0.00	0.848	0.77	0.701*	1.83
Diabetes	0.720	0.83	0.867	0.38	0.434**	2.15	0.845	0.39	0.523	1.52
Hypertension	1.230	0.62	0.805	0.61	0.993	0.02	1.563	1.11	1.247	0.59
Heart disease	0.632	0.83	1.795	1.26	1.612	1.05	0.346*	1.90	0.900	0.23
Stroke	0.907	0.14	2.220	1.21	0.355	1.33	0.416	1.28	0.152**	2.38
Pseudo R²	0.06						0.07			
N	12,190						8,782			

Source: World Bank.

Note: The table shows adjusted odds ratios (AORs) from a logistic model. The binary dependent variable is whether a respondent is likely to have a respiratory infection as calculated using relevant symptoms (using a 14-day recall) and methods outlined in Appendix B Table B.2. Analysis of heterogeneity across study sites is reported for selected demographic characteristics and comorbidities with the comparator site and major construction and persistent traffic as the base category. Results are restricted to persistent traffic, major construction and traffic, and brick kiln sites. Robust standard errors are calculated using the Huber–White (1967) approach methods. Results are also interpretable as percentage changes ([AOR – 1] * 100 = percentage change).

***, **, and * represent significance below the 1 percent, 5 percent, and 10 percent levels.

TABLE B.12 Means tests of depression, by location and demographic characteristics (14-day recall)

PERSISTENT TRAFFIC VERSUS COMPARATOR	MAJOR CONSTRUCTION AND TRAFFIC VERSUS COMPARATOR	BRICK KILNS VERSUS COMPARATOR	PERSISTENT TRAFFIC VERSUS BRICK KILNS	MAJOR CONSTRUCTION AND TRAFFIC VERSUS BRICK KILNS
See figure 3.17				
..	..	..	**	**
See figure 3.18				

0–5 YEARS VERSUS 6–19 YEARS	0–5 YEARS VERSUS 20–64 YEARS	0–5 YEARS VERSUS 65+ YEARS	MALE VERSUS FEMALE
**	***	***	*

Source: World Bank.
Note: Prevalence of depression has been determined using the WHO-5 depression screening tool. Test statistics are derived using standard *t*-tests.
***, **, and * represent significance below the 1 percent, 5 percent, and 10 percent levels.

TABLE B.13 Correlates of depression (14-day recall)

	ADJUSTED ODDS RATIOS	STANDARD ERROR
Base: Comparator		
Persistent traffic	1.050	0.40
Major construction and traffic	0.955	0.37
Brick kilns	0.762**	2.46
$PM_{2.5}$	1.202***	3.79
PM_{10}	1.017	0.35
Base: Age 15–35 years		
36–49 years	1.069	0.68
50–64 years	1.395***	3.10
65+	2.871***	7.95
Female (base: male)	1.357***	3.80
Improved fuel (base: unimproved)	0.897	1.16
Household size	1.027	1.10
Hours spent outdoors	1.032***	3.71
Base: Poorest		
Poor	0.835*	1.69
Mid	0.736***	2.82
Rich	0.637***	3.93
Richest	0.583***	4.37
Education (base: none)		
Primary	0.601***	4.59
Secondary	0.673***	4.32
High school	0.615***	2.91
High school and above	0.637**	2.11
Religious education	0.391*	1.85
Allergies	1.082	0.91
Diabetes	1.134	0.91
Hypertension	1.251**	2.06
Heart disease	1.377**	1.97

continued

TABLE B.13, *continued*

	ADJUSTED ODDS RATIOS	STANDARD ERROR
Stroke	2.772***	4.45
Cough (short term)	1.089	0.58
Breathing problems (short term)	1.561***	3.01
Fever (short term)	1.217**	2.05
Respiratory infection (short term)	1.263	1.36
Pseudo R²	0.070	
N	8,034	

Source: World Bank.
Note: The table shows adjusted odds ratios (AORs) from a logistic model. The binary dependent variable is whether a respondent is depressed as per the WHO-5 scale. Robust standard errors are calculated using the Huber-White (Huber 1967) approach. Results are interpretable as percentage changes ([AOR – 1] * 100 = percentage change). PM = particulate matter. PM numbers indicate the size of the particles. PM_1 indicates particles of 1 micrometer, and so forth.
***, **, and * represent significance below the 1 percent, 5 percent, and 10 percent levels.

MAP B.1

Location of continuous air-monitoring stations in Bangladesh

Source: Based on information from the Department of Environment, Ministry of Environment, Forest, and Climate Change.
Note: Two additional continuous air-monitoring stations (CAMS) were set up in 2019/2020—in Rangpur and Mymensingh—not shown in the map. The location of the CAMS are as follows: CAMS-1 Dhaka Sangshad Bhaban Shere-Bangla Nagar; CAMS-2 Dhaka Firmgate; CAMS-3 Dhaka Darus Salam; CAMS-4 Gazipur; CAMS-5 Narayangonj; CAMS-6 Chattogram TV Station Khulshi; CAMS-7 Chattogram Agrabad; CAMS-8 Khulna Baira; CAMS-9 Rajshahi Sopura; CAMS-10 Sylhet Red Crescent Campus; and CAMS-11 Barishal DFO Office Campus (Clean Air and Sustainable Environment Project 2018).

FIGURE B.1

Pollutant levels in outdoor conditions (natural units), by study site

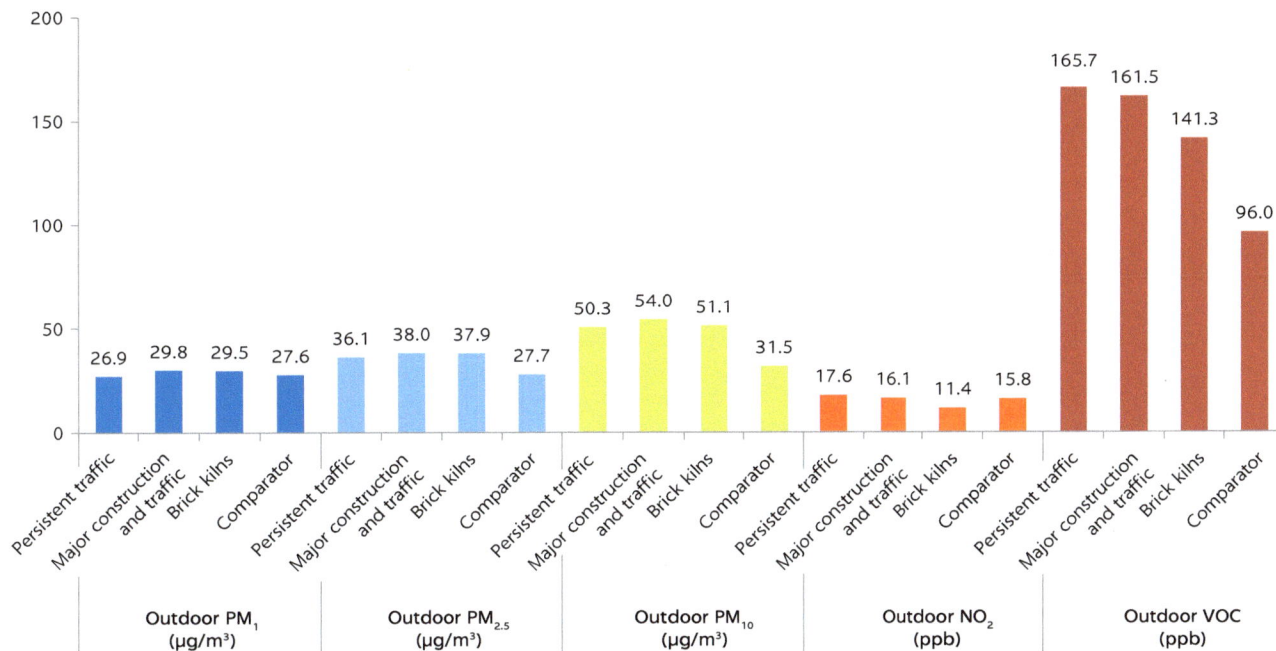

Source: World Bank.
Note: PM = particulate matter. PM numbers indicate the size of particles: PM$_1$ indicates particles of 1 micrometer, and so forth. NO$_2$ = nitrogen dioxide. ppb = parts per billion. μg/m³ = micrograms per cubic meter. VOC = volatile organic compound.

FIGURE B.2

Pollutant levels in indoor conditions, by study site

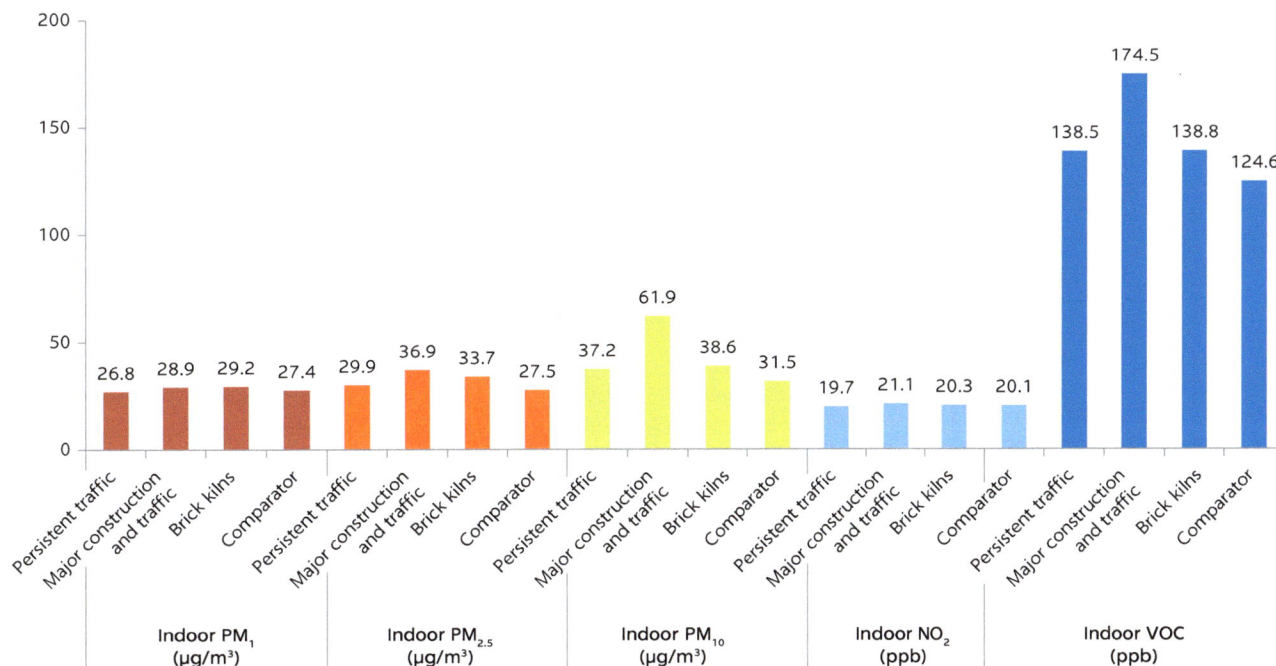

Source: World Bank.
Note: PM = particulate matter. PM numbers indicate the size of particles: PM$_1$ indicates particles of 1 micrometer, and so forth. NO$_2$ = nitrogen dioxide. ppb = parts per billion. μg/m³ = micrograms per cubic meter. VOC = volatile organic compound.

Pollutant levels in outdoor and indoor conditions, by study site

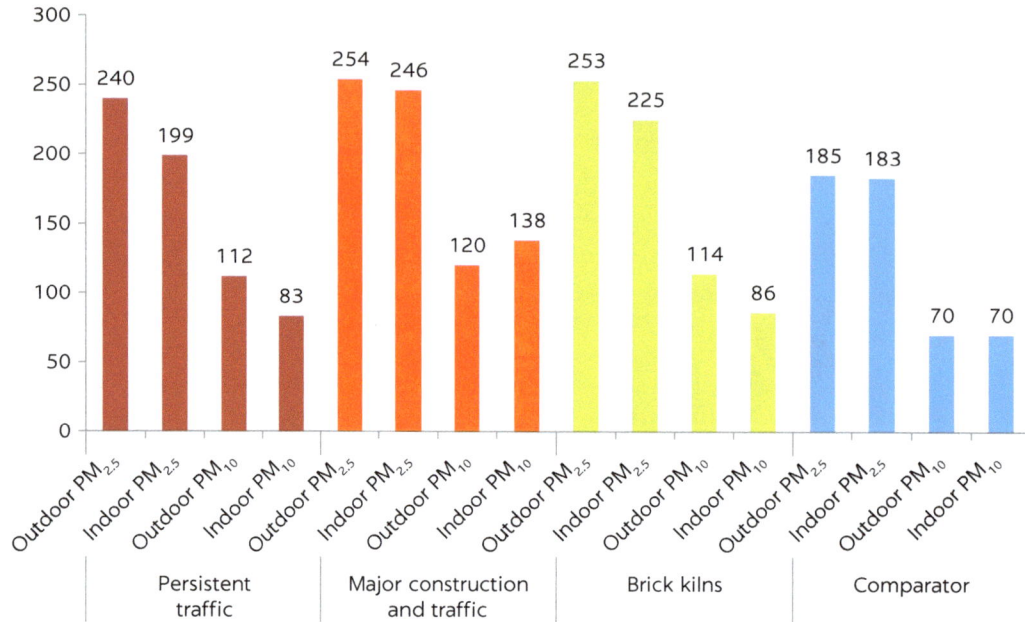

Source: World Bank.
Note: PM = particulate matter. PM numbers indicate the size of particles: PM_1 indicates particles of 1 micrometer, and so forth. PMs are presented as a percentage above (or below) the World Health Organization's 2021 Air Quality Guidelines over a 24-hour period (see glossary).

REFERENCES

Clean Air and Sustainable Environment Project. 2018. *Monthly Air Quality Monitoring Report, Reporting Month: July, 2018*. Dhaka: Bangladesh Department of Environment.

Huber, P. 1967. "The Behavior of Maximum Likelihood Estimates under Nonstandard Conditions." *Proceedings of the Fifth Berkeley Symposium on Mathematical Statistics and Probability*. Vol. 5: 221–33.

Variables and Analytical Technique

SURVEY INSTRUMENT AND VARIABLES

The structured questionnaire administered during the survey comprised both individual- and household-level questions. Individual-level questions were directed at each member of the household. For members below 10 years of age, the mother or primary caregiver furnished the requisite information. The primary female member of the household responded to household-level questions.

The primary questions of interest revolved around the individual's physical and mental health conditions. On physical health, self-reported information was collected on two fronts. Based on available literature and using a 14-day recall period, we collected short-term symptoms of exposure to air pollution such as experiencing a cough or breathing difficulties; fever; redness, burning sensations, wateriness, or itchiness of the eyes; nasal issues such as runniness and/or blockage, whether accompanied by headaches, itchiness, dryness, or general irritation; rashes, hives, itching, acne, or dermatitis on the skin; and soreness, pain or ache, itchiness, or dryness of the throat. The information related to cough is further detailed through additional questions related to whether the cough was productive (inclusive of sputum), the consistency and color of the sputum, and the presence of blood. The information on breathing difficulties was further qualified depending on whether the individual hears a wheezing sound when breathing. In consultation with trained medical professionals, a scoring mechanism was developed to predict whether an individual was experiencing a respiratory infection using a series of cascading questions. The questions and relevant score, including the cutoff, are detailed in appendix B, table B.2. Next, using a 12-month recall, the questionnaire also accumulated individual-level illness data on a battery of both communicable and noncommunicable diseases that were confirmed to have been diagnosed by a trained physician.

Mental health was measured using the five-item World Health Organization Well-Being Index (WHO-5), which is an instrument comprising five simple, noninvasive questions designed to assess subjective psychological well-being. Since its creation in 1998, the WHO-5 has been translated into more than 30 languages and has been widely used in research studies globally (Topp et al. 2015). The scale consists of a Likert-style questionnaire, with the highest possible score of 100 representing perfect well-being. Topp et al.'s (2015) comprehensive systematic review of studies (n = 18) utilizing the WHO-5 demonstrated the instrument to have high clinical validity. The review indicated that a score threshold of ≤ 50 has utility in assigning a "screening diagnosis" of depression, with a sensitivity of 0.87 and specificity of 0.76. A Bangla version of the WHO-5 has recently been culturally adapted (internal consistency: α = 0.754) and validated against previously validated instruments in Bangladesh (divergent validity: r = −0.443, p < 0.01 with the Bangla version of Perceived Stress Scale-10; and convergent validity: r = 0.542, p < 0.01 with the Bangla version of Warwick-Edinburgh Mental Well-Being Scale) using rigorous transcultural translation and validation procedures (Faruk et al. 2021). Accordingly, the study uses the Bangla version of the WHO-5 with an operationalized cutoff of ≤ 50 to determine populations with a screening diagnosis of depression.

Additional individual-level information includes a roster comprising demographic, educational, and occupational characteristics as well as time-use with regard to the average number of hours spent in air-conditioned and non-air-conditioned environments and outdoors on a typical day. The survey collated information on an additional array of individual and household characteristics. A composite socioeconomic index, accounting for survey-site specific characteristics, was created from physical household attributes— wall and roof material, area per capita, and availability of a separate kitchen— and a roster of durable assets was created using methods outlined in the Bangladesh Demographic and Health Survey (NIPORT and ICF 2020). Quintiles of the continuous index are used for analysis. Information was also collected on whether the household used improved sources of energy for cooking along with water, sanitation, and hygiene (WaSH) attributes such as accessibility to sanitary facilities, type of water used, hygiene-oriented behavior such as hand washing, and others.

ANALYTICAL TECHNIQUES

This paper models the correlates of physical and mental health outcomes reported in sections "Correlates of productive cough, breathing difficulties, and respiratory infections" and "Correlates of depression," using the following binary specification:

$$Y_{ij} = \frac{e^{\beta_1\omega_j + \beta_2\gamma_{ij} + \Phi'\mathrm{P} + X'\psi + \Theta'\Upsilon + \varepsilon_{ij}}}{1 + e^{\beta_1\omega_j + \beta_2\gamma_{ij} + \Phi'\mathrm{P} + X'\psi + \Theta'\Upsilon + \varepsilon_{ij}}}$$

$$i = 1\ldots n$$
$$j = 0\ldots 100,$$

(C.1)

where the probability of binary outcome Y = 1 is modeled for the ith individual living in the jth primary sampling unit. The study sites[1] (with the comparator location as the base category) and the particulate matter are denoted by ω_j and γ_{ij}. Φ' represents a vector of demographic characteristics such as age and gender, while the set of comorbidities is denoted by X'. Θ' represents a vector of individual- and household-level characteristics such as usual activity and socioeconomic status, time use and so forth. ε_{ij} is the Huber-White (1967) robust idiosyncratic error term.

The study hypothesizes that variation and composition of the pollutant particles will vary by each study site and have differential effects, particularly across demographic characteristics and in the presence of comorbidities across each of the study sites. To assess the heterogeneity of effects, we extend equation C.1 to have the study sites to interact with the two sets of attributes:

$$Y_{ij} = \frac{e^{\beta_1 \omega_j + \beta_2 \gamma_{ij} + \Phi' P + X' \Psi + \gamma^*(\Phi')\beta_3 + \gamma^*(X')\beta_4 + \Theta' \Upsilon + \varepsilon_{ij}}}{1 + e^{\beta_1 \omega_j + \beta_2 \gamma_{ij} + \Phi' P + X' \Psi + \gamma^*(\Phi')\beta_3 + \gamma^*(X')\beta_4 + \Theta' \Upsilon + \varepsilon_{ij}}} \tag{C.2}$$
$$i = 1 \ldots n$$
$$j = 0 \ldots 100,$$

where the coefficients of the interacted terms (β_3 and β_4) represent the differential effects on demographic characteristics and comorbidities between the study sites 1 through 3 against the comparator. A second set of results are derived using equation B.2, where study sites 1 and 3 are benchmarked against site 2 for comparison.

The results presented are adjusted odds ratios (AORs) and can be interpreted as percentage changes.[2] All analysis was conducted using STATA v17.1 and Tableau 2021.8.4.

NOTES

1. Study sites include persistent traffic, major construction and traffic, brick kilns, and comparator.
2. (AOR – 1) * 100 = percentage change. For example, an AOR of 1.66 is interpretable as a 66 percent increase over the base category.

REFERENCES

Faruk, M.O., F. Alam, K. U. A. Chowdhury, and T. R. Soron. 2021. "Validation of the Bangla WHO-5 Well-Being Index." *Global Mental Health* (Cambodia) 8: e26.

Huber, P. J. 1967. "The Behavior of Maximum Likelihood Estimates under Nonstandard Conditions." *Proceedings of the Fifth Berkeley Symposium on Mathematical Statistics and Probability* 5: 221–33.

NIPORT (National Institute of Population Research and Training) and ICF. 2020. "Bangladesh Demographic and Health Survey 2017–18." Dhaka, Bangladesh, and Rockville, Maryland. NIPORT and ICF.

Topp, C. W., S. D. Østergaard, S. Søndergaard, and P. Bech. 2015. "The WHO-5 Well-Being Index: A Systematic Review of the Literature." *Psychotherapy and Psychosomatics* 84 (3): 167–76.

www.ingramcontent.com/pod-product-compliance
Lightning Source LLC
Chambersburg PA
CBHW060813270326
41929CB00002B/24

Larabee, his widow, March 2001